T0375203

THE ADVENT OVERTURE

Meditations and Poems for the Christmas Season

Stuart McAlpine

WESTBOW
PRESS®
A DIVISION OF THOMAS NELSON
& ZONDERVAN

Cover design: Pete Berg Graphics

WestBow Press books may be ordered through booksellers or by contacting:

WestBow Press
A Division of Thomas Nelson & Zondervan
1663 Liberty Drive
Bloomington, IN 47403
www.westbowpress.com
1 (866) 928-1240

ISBN: 978-1-9736-1011-3 (sc)
ISBN: 978-1-9736-1012-0 (hc)
ISBN: 978-1-9736-1010-6 (e)

Library of Congress Control Number: 2017917342

Print information available on the last page.

WestBow Press rev. date: 11/28/2014

To three generations of my family with whom I share Christmas joys: Celia, Charis, Seulgi, Noah, Maliya, Micah, Caleb, Ewen, Jemimah, Esme, Jonas, Gavin, Zeke, Christa, Tim, Ailyn, Tighe, Brendan, Laurel, Adeline, Alys, Luke.

To all the sheep who have ever been in the pasture known as Christ Our Shepherd Church in Washington D.C. with whom I have shared the celebration of The Advent Overture for thirty years with its "good news of great joy."

Contents

* This font indicates poems

Logos

"The Word became flesh."
(John 1:14)

Father,
They say that penmanship reveals the man.
We scribe and others read the hidden soul.
They say that once you wrote a single word;
That swaddled vellum fast-bound all your life.
Please dip your quill into my inked heart's well,
And grace-stroke once again that word in me ...
Jesus.

"Christ is in me."
(2 Corinthians 11:10)

(1984)

1

The Advent Overture

The English word, 'overture', comes from the French word 'ouverture' which means 'opening'. The overture comes at the opening of the main work, and is a term used most commonly for a piece of music. The many elements that it contains are foreshadowing what is to come: the themes that will be amplified later on in the unveiling of the musical or written script.

The gospel narratives that describe the birth of Jesus are the overture of the New Testament. It is one of the richest veins of scripture for its revelation of who God is, what God does, and why and how He does it. Like an overture, the opening account of the incarnation contains within it the notes of gospel truth and discipleship that are going to be developed in all that follows, whether in the gospels or in the epistles. So by way of introduction, it would be good to identify some of these important themes and tune our ears to them so they prepare us for their repeated strains throughout the New Testament.

Was That Natural or Normal?
It was not. The frequency of the *supernatural activity of the Holy Spirit* in these Advent events is breath-taking. All the crucial instructions and directions to Joseph were in dreams: "The Lord appeared to him in a dream" (Matthew 1:20; 2:13; 2:19; 2:22). The wise men were "warned in a dream" (Matthew 2:12). There were angels everywhere. "An angel of the Lord appeared to Joseph" (Matthew 1:20); "an angel of the Lord appeared to Zechariah" (Luke 1:11); "God sent the angel Gabriel … to a virgin" (Luke 1:26); "an angel of the Lord appeared" to shepherds (Luke 2:9); "A great company of the heavenly host appeared" (Luke 2:13). There was a supernatural movement in the cosmos as a star moved into place. Did that star just get specially created for the occasion or was it the light of a star

2

that God made millennia before, which had already burned out but whose light and movement were precision-fixed before Adam was even thought of? Any way you look at it, it is awesome.

There is a supernatural sign given, as Zechariah is struck dumb. This is attention grabbing to say the least, especially for Zechariah. There is a miraculous fertilization of Elizabeth's womb and does it not say she was filled with the Holy Spirit (Luke 1:42)? John was baptized in the Holy Spirit at the same time in his mother's womb and did a charismatic somersault. Elizabeth had a word of knowledge, a gift of the Holy Spirit, in naming her son John. Then there was a pregnancy without any human insemination. Gabriel told Mary that it would be the Holy Spirit that would come upon her, surely the most unique experience of the Holy Spirit any human being has ever had. She would be with child "through the Holy Spirit." Without that supernatural dream, how do you think Joseph would have responded to Mary's news that the Holy Spirit did it? Zechariah's dumbness was supernaturally healed; he is filled with the Holy Spirit and prophesies. Previously through Mary, there had been an extraordinary supernatural manifestation of the gift of prophecy that we know as the Magnificat.

Of Simeon it says that the Holy Spirit was upon him and that what he knew was revealed by the Holy Spirit. He and Anna happened to be at exactly the right place at the right time after decades of asking: they entered the temple, and turned the corner right on cue. Why? Because the text says of Simeon, "moved by the Spirit he went" (Luke 2:27). Anna was equally wind-blown by the Spirit. The text says "at that very moment" (Luke 2:38). The whole story is Holy Spirit saturated.

How does Advent season find us? Are we feeling dry, directionless, disconnected to the heart of God and the mind of Christ, distant, depleted, unexpectant or joyless? The principle remains the same: without the Holy Spirit coming upon us, Jesus is not formed in us. The text is telling us that like all these characters, we may need, and we can have, a fresh encounter with the Holy Spirit.

Glory Here, There and Everywhere

There is an *explosion of worship* in this story that is enough to fuel the exhilarations of any and every praise gathering. "My soul glorifies the Lord and my spirit rejoices in God my Savior," exclaimed Mary. "The Lord has done great things for me," testified Elizabeth. "Praise be to the God of Israel," exhorted Zechariah. "Glory to God in the highest," announced the angelic host. The shepherds are described as "glorifying and praising God for all the things they had seen and heard." The wise men "worshiped and opened their treasures". When Simeon saw Jesus he "took him in his arms and praised God." Anna "worshiped night and day" and she "gave thanks to God and spoke about the child."

What is our worship this Advent? Has familiarity dulled our worship? Has formality suppressed our praise? Has loss of intimacy evaporated our vocabulary of love, and has diminished expectation quenched our joy? The text invites us to recover our wide-eyed wonder at the grace and generosity of God, to reconnect with the one who came to save us, and whose salvation is the catalyst for unbridled thanksgiving.

Stop and Go

The birth narratives present the necessary *relationship between "waiting" on God and for Him, and "hastening" in obedience to Him* when He speaks and gives directions. There is a time to tarry and a time to hurry, just as there is a word that waits and a word that is immediate. We always want God to be in a hurry. "Make haste to help us!" Psalms 22, 38, 40 and 70 are psalms that we identify with, though there is an interesting warning: "Woe to those who tell God to make speed and hasten His work" (Isaiah 5:19). We see Elizabeth waiting on God as she hides herself for five months. When Mary stays with Elizabeth in secret for three of those months, she too waits on the Lord. Simeon is waiting for the consolation of Israel and Anna is waiting night and day. There is the waiting for the promises and the Word to be fulfilled, the things that were "said through His prophets of long ago" (Luke 1:10) and the words that would "come true at the proper time" (Luke 1:20).

But then there were the appropriate obedient responses to the Word: of a Mary who "hurried" (Luke 1:39), and of shepherds who "hastened" (Luke 2:16). There are so many examples of what Psalm 119:60 speaks about: "I made haste and did not delay to keep your commandments." Joseph is told in a dream to "Get up!" His obedience was immediate. "So he got up and took the child and his mother during the night" (Matthew 2:13-14). He did not wait for the dawn when it would have been safer.

What is our posture and pace this Advent? Are we in a headlong hurry, without consulting the Lord's Word or will for our lives and direction? Are we in danger of acting presumptuously rather than prayerfully? Are we tempted to be pragmatic rather than principled? It is so easy to be driven by necessity or need, instead of being led by the Holy Spirit. Perhaps we are in a weakened state, emotionally and spiritually or physically and the Word of the Lord to us is "those who wait on the Lord will renew their strength" (Isaiah 40:31). Maybe we need to wait on the Lord this Advent.

Equally, how often do we drag our feet over a matter of holy obedience? Maybe like Zechariah our problem is that we have failed to hasten when we received the Word of the Lord. A sense of immediacy is evident in these narratives as the participants respond to the will of God. Is that a present need in a specific area of our lives? Do we need a fresh obedient spring in our step? In 1 Samuel 21:8 we read: "The king's business requires haste." Let the Advent story speak to us, both about tarrying and hurrying.

It's All about Jesus

If there was no other text of the New Testament, the first chapter of Luke would be sufficient in giving us an amazing summary of *the work and person of Christ*, provoking our expectations of salvation and deliverance. The nature of the gospel and the nature of Jesus Christ are writ large in this script, as well as in Matthew's account:

- He will save his people from their sins (Matthew 1:21).
- He will be the presence of God with us (Matthew 1:23).
- He will be both a ruler and a shepherd (Matthew 1:26).
- He will have power and authority to reign (Luke 1:33).
- He is the Son of God (Luke 1:35).
- He will redeem (Luke 1:68).
- He will rescue (Luke 1:74).
- He will enable (Luke 1:74).
- He will show mercy (Luke 1:72).

- He will forgive (Luke 1:77).
- He is the Lord, the Messiah (Luke 2:11, 26).
- He is salvation (Luke 2:30).
- He is light (Luke 2:30).
- He is revelation to the Gentiles (Luke 2:30).
- He is glory to the Jews (Luke 2:30).
- He will expose and reveal hearts (Luke 2:35).
- He will suffer (Luke 2:34).

Perhaps our greatest need this Advent is a reminder of who Jesus is and why He came. This is not about coming to a crib but coming to the Christ. Of which of these extraordinary revelations of Jesus do we need to avail ourselves? Is it salvation, forgiveness of sin, rescue, mercy, revelation, or comfort? All are available to be received and appropriated. Perhaps we need Him as the exposer of our hearts, as the ruler of our lives, as the shepherd of our souls, as the light of our paths. Is this what the text is inviting us to?

Promises, Promises

These narratives are a lesson in *the promises of God*. As someone put it: "When the questions have no answers, the promises remain." They reveal the character of the God who gives the promise, the content of God's Word about what is promised, the concern of God's love for those who will receive the promise and the consequences of God's actions in the lives of those who experience the fulfillment of the promises. You have to acknowledge that this incarnation narrative came out of the blue, or out of the black more likely. For the second time in their national experience Israel had endured four centuries of darkness and captivity. If the first captivity of Israel was slavery, then this last one was imprisonment by silence. Spiritual incarceration preceded spiritual incarnation. The problem was worse than unanswered. It was unanswered because God seemed absent. It was silent, not just because God was not speaking, but because it felt like He was not there to hear.

As the 400 years of silence lapped right up to Zechariah's feet as he stood at that altar of incense, mouthing the same old liturgical prayers for deliverance, over 300 prophetic-promises of the Messiah's coming insisted on breaking through loud and clear "in the fullness of time."

Did not Gabriel say to Zechariah that his words would come true "at the proper time"? This becomes the narrative's refrain. Prior promises are being fulfilled: "remembering to be merciful to Abraham and his descendants … as He said through His prophets long ago … to remember His holy covenant" (Luke 1: 54-55; 1:70: 1:72). The narrative teaches us that there is a way from His past promise to present praise, even though we have to pass through the problems and the pain.

Maybe this is what we need to hear this Advent. God's covenant love for us is not absent even though we wait for His deliverance. The promise that is unfulfilled is not negated by the lack of a present answer. We have a history and a narrative of His faithfulness and trustworthiness. Even our past sin that broke covenant has not separated us from His covenant love. Truly, when the questions have no answers the promises remain.

Bringing Reality into the Presence of God

The gospel birth narratives are texts that do not shy away from the *realities of personal life* and of national history. Not surprisingly, they present so many stark threats. It is a story about real problems, that does not judge the difficulties, the obstacles, the pains and the suffering, but wherever you look, there seems to be a crisis. It is national (the occupation of the Romans), religious (there is no prophetic word and no sense of God's presence), and personal (there are babies that are both longed for and unplanned). There are words that suddenly appear like razor-sharp reefs, threatening to sink and drown faith and fulfillment, words like: barren, fear, dumbness, silence, divorce, troubled, shame, disgrace, reproach, sword, Herod, and weeping. Indeed, there was adoration but there was also assassination. There seemed to be as much bad news as good news.

Is this what we need to know? Like the characters in the story, we too can bring the reality of our lives into the presence of God, and come just as we are, with all the problems, all the contradictions and confusions, all the fears and unbelief and all the disqualifying circumstances of our lives. God includes us in the narrative of His plan and purposes anyway. The problems are not enough to deny us a prospect in God's redemptive purposes. Problems are overcome and overwhelmed in this story by the grace of God, as are ours, when grace is allowed to re-clothe us and remove the garments of our stained shame and disabling self-consciousness.

Magnify

Then there is the Magnificat (Luke 1:46-55), a spiritual Magna Carta in its own right about *the nature of the kingdom of God.* This is a concentrate of teaching describing a moral revolution (scattering of the proud), a social revolution (casting down rulers and lifting up the humble) and an economic revolution (filling the hungry with good things). Nowhere in the New Testament outside the teaching of Jesus Himself is there such a clear manifesto that deals with the precedents for God's anticipated kingdom actions, and it is coming out of the mouth of a teenage girl. All of our prime-time journalists would have interviewed all the wrong people. Someone has described this as one of the most revolutionary documents in the world, for good reason. It is a hymn to the universal authority of Christ who is bringing total renewal. Mary is describing the supernatural break-in, breakthrough and breakout of the kingdom of God, and there is not a professional theologian in sight. All the precedents of former divine actions combine with all the present experiences of divine intervention; all the promises of the past combine with all the prospects of a future deliverance.

The New Testament opens with a reconnection with the Psalms that magnify God and sing their messianic expectation. Psalmic language laces the Magnificat, as well as the Benedictus (Zechariah's song of thanksgiving in Luke 1:68-79) and the Nunc Dimmitis (Simeon's song of praise in Luke 2:29-32). Together, these three canticles provide the worship-overture for the gospel. The opening blessing of the Benedictus is the closing blessing of three Psalter books. Mary's vocabulary is even more Psalm-soaked and seeped than Zechariah's (Psalm 34:1-3; 105; 107; 146). The Magnificat declares that what the psalmists continually hoped and prayed for, especially justice for the poor and the humbling of the proud, was now being realized and fulfilled in Jesus.

Will we be encouraged by this good news this Advent? God is working His purposes out. The kingdom of God is advancing and growing and it will be established in justice and righteousness. We need to be assured and affirmed by the nature of this kingdom that we have been brought into. It is glorious. Let us take stock of our co-ordinates and be reminded of the true spiritual geography in which we live.

As He Said

It is impossible to miss *the centrality of God's Word* in these texts, as it both reveals and releases God's will. Two things are foundational to Luke's presentation: the heavenly revelation of the Word (both prophetic and angelic) and the human response to the Word. The sluice gates of the prophetic witness swing open and the words of Isaiah and Micah, of Hosea and Jeremiah, pour out like they were spoken just yesterday. The relationship between the Word given ("it is written … the angel said … this took place to fulfill what was said") and the Word obeyed ("he did as the Lord commanded … let it be done to me") is a tutorial in discipleship. The word of the Lord is like a wave that crashes on to the shore of their lives and leaves them all saturated: "according to your word … as you have promised … as He said to our fathers … as He said through the holy prophets." The contrast between the passion of Mary's song and the dumb silence of Zechariah is simply the difference between two contrary responses to the Word.

How are we responding to God's Word this Advent? Jesus' ministry begins in the gospels with this appeal: "He who has ears to hear, let him hear" (Mark 4:9). It ends with exactly the same words to the seven churches of Asia Minor (Revelation 2:7). It is all about hearing His Word and listening to what it says. It was Jesus Himself who gave us the clearest idea about how our response to the Word affected the outcomes of our lives. Is our hearing stony and impenetrable? Is it rocky, superficially hearing but more an itching ear than an attentive one? Is it thorny, succumbing to competing demands for attention, and the allure of other voices? This Advent let us apprehend and apply the Word from this incarnation narrative.

Ask and Keep on Asking

"The assembled worshippers were praying outside … your prayers have been heard … Simeon … was waiting for the consolation of Israel … Anna … worshiped night and day, fasting and praying" (Luke 1:10, 13; 2:25-38). The emphasis on prayer is overwhelming. After all, the opening words of this story are: "Your prayers have been answered!" (1:13) That means that prior to this communication, there must have been a lot of asking. You could teach countless lessons about prayer without ever leaving this text. It is about who we pray to and about why we pray, even if there is a long delay. It is about how to respond to both answers and lack of answers. It is about intercession with fasting. It is about persevering prayer over decades. It is about longing prayers over centuries. Above all, it is about prayer that gets not what we want, but what God wants. Have you ever considered that? Prayer is about getting what God wants for us, more than what we want for ourselves.

Does our asking of God need some encouragement this Advent? Has our asking been eroded? Is it discouraged? Like many in the story, are there just too many unanswered prayers to deal with? Has persistence been abandoned? Jesus had so much to say about asking of His Father, so maybe this Advent, this story of prayer will take us from the overture to the teaching of Jesus about asking that we find in the gospels.

The Good Shepherd

We have noted many of the themes and threads of these narratives but what is particularly evident about this story is its *pastoral power,* as we identify with the attitudes and emotions of the characters in their interactions with God and each other. Yes, there are shepherds in the story, but the Chief Shepherd is God Himself, crooking and flocking the characters into the pasture of His purposes and provisions. So much can be learned through them about how God can recover order where there has been chaos, not just in the historic sense on the grand stage of history, but in the personal sense, as we get insight into the delicacy of the Spirit's work in households, in marriages, in family relationships. We watch as God takes people from a place of disintegration in personal life to a place of recovered integrity. He seems to specialize in seeking and finding the sheep that are lost.

We find people in the story just like us. Most of them are not ready to be used by God let alone found by Him. They are overwhelmed by the excluding clauses of their natural state. They are all too "something or other". When found they are thinking that the conditions of their life and circumstances maybe too late, too impossible, too embarrassing, too shameful, or just too bad and too sad. But out of these same mouths, breaking the silence, come cries. From the one who is past-it comes, "His name is John"; from the one who was ready to get a divorce lawyer, "His name is Jesus"; from the one who was looking like the village tart, "all generations will call me blessed"; from the one who had waited a lifetime, "my eyes have seen your salvation."

This Advent, do we need to take strength and succor from any of their testimonies? All the facts of our lives, all our actions, words and thoughts that seem to contradict the revelation of Christ, even oppose it, are equally embraced by grace, and we realize personally that indeed nothing is impossible for God. And if He can take them and include them in the most incredible story ever lived, He can equally take us and assure us that by His Spirit we too can have what it takes to become players in the divine theater of God's purposes.

The Advent Overture
Indeed, there are so many melodies in the Advent Overture, but what follows in this book is focused on the preceding point: the sheer pastoral power of this story to speak to where we are, as we find ourselves relating to the responses of the characters to the circumstances of their lives. Time and time again, you will hear chords of love and truth that will be repeated in the gospels and epistles that follow. The incarnation story could not be a better one for whetting your appetite for what follows in the rest of the New Testament.

As we listen to the Advent Overture that follows, it will be alternatively poetic and meditative. For over thirty years I have committed myself every Advent to meditate on the text and to write a poem that is inspired by what I have heard and learned "according to His Word". All the characters in the story have become my spiritual mentors. I offer this Overture to you as an encouragement to you to keep listening to the full symphony of God's work in Jesus Christ. Advent blessings to you and yours!

What Has Straw to Do with Grain?

"Let's make bricks ... it was called Babel ... Let the one who has
my word speak it faithfully. For what has straw to do with grain?"
(Genesis 11: 3-9; Jeremiah 23:28)

Babylon
Mortared aspiration
Straw-bricks skyward vaulting
Heaven's gate assaulting
Man's oven-ready lust is kilned in vain
And cannot entrance into glory gain

Bethlehem
Mangered incarnation
Straw-stalks earth-bound lying
Heaven's access crying
The kerneled wheat in swaddling husk was lain
Consider ... what has straw to do with grain?

"Unless a kernel of wheat falls into the ground and dies it
remains alone. But if it dies it produces many seeds."
(John 12:24)
(1985)

First Things First

The observance of Advent is a Christian practice that celebrates the incarnation: the fact that Christ was born, the truth that God became man. However, 'adventus' (Latin for 'coming') has always been associated with both the preparation for celebrating incarnation, as well as the anticipation of the Parousia, the Second Coming of Christ. Liturgically, Advent has a long history. Some historians argue that the first mention of it can be traced to the Council of Sargossa in 380AD, but by the time of the Council of Tours (563AD) and Mâcon (581AD) liturgical practices for Advent are assumed given the practical suggestions for advent preparations that were presented at these gatherings.

The Gentile Christian celebration of Advent has well-known traditions that have been influenced by any number of pagan Gentile ones. The Christianization of a pagan festival inevitably involved the adoption of some of the original features. For example, the history of the Christmas tree, though it includes suggestions that it developed from the Paradise Tree in the Garden of Eden, is most likely the evergreen fir that was commonly used in pagan religion to celebrate winter and the winter solstice. The Romans used it to decorate their pagan temples at the Festival of Saturnalia, the false worship of their deity Saturn. It is strongly argued that the reason that Christians chose December 25th was because it was the birthday of two powerfully opposing false deities: Zeus the Greek god, and Jupiter the Roman one.

Christmas, for obvious reasons, is clearly not a Jewish celebration. The seasonal Jewish feast that is closest to Christmas in timing is Hanukkah, celebrating the re-dedication of the Second Temple after the Maccabean Revolt against the blasphemies of Antiochus. It happens sometime between the end of November and the end of December because it is based on the lunar calendar, so Hanukkah cards and Christmas cards can always be found in stores at the same time. Like Christmas, it is has a strong family appeal, and involves candles (thus also known as the Festival of Lights) and there is also the exchange of gifts. Like Christmas, when we pray the Christmas Collects, it has particular prayers to express thanksgiving, one of them being the 'Al-ha-Nissum' ('about miracles'). The opening words could well be those of a Christian prayer of thanksgiving for Yeshua's birth: "We thank you also for the miraculous deeds and for the redemption and for the mighty deeds and the saving acts wrought by you."

So what is the point? Sadly, precisely because Christmas is Gentile, most people are likely to go through Advent season without so much as a thought for a fundamental incarnational truth. Read the following from the birth narratives and you will understand: "A record of the genealogy of Jesus Christ *the son of David, the son of Abraham* ... He will save *His people* from their sins ... Where is the one who has been born *King of the Jews* ... out of you will come a ruler who will be the shepherd of *my people Israel* ... The Lord will give Him the throne of *His father David* and He will rule over *the house of Jacob* ... He has helped *His servant Israel*, remembering to be merciful to *Abraham and his descendants* forever ... Praise be to the Lord the *God of Israel* because He has come and has redeemed *His people Israel* ... to remember His holy covenant, the oath He swore to our *Father Abraham* ... in *the town of David* a Savior has been born to you ... to offer a sacrifice in keeping with what is said in *the law of the Lord* ... for glory to *your people Israel* ... the child is destined to cause the falling and rising of many *in Israel*" (Matthew 1:1; 1:21; 2:6; Luke 1:32; 1:54-55; 1:68; 1:72-73; 2:11; 2: 22-24; 2:32; 2:34).

Did anything stand out? Did you have any thoughts or conclusions? The New Testament opens in a Jewish world, geographically and spiritually. The events are in Jerusalem, in Nazareth and the Judean hill country. Key exchanges take place in the Temple and it is about the religion of Judaism, its religious practices and its law. The only people in Luke's story who are looking for the "hope of Israel" are Jews. Our initial engagement with the birth narratives has been compared to the experience of landing at an airport where everything is only written in Hebrew without any translations for anyone else. So where are the specific mentions of Gentiles?

There are two key references to Abraham and to what he had been promised when God made covenant with him (Luke 1:54-55; 1:72-73). Zechariah's song confirms that what is happening is "to remember His holy covenant." What has that got to do with Gentiles? What is subsumed in that covenant is the promise that "all peoples on earth will be blessed through you" (Genesis 12:3). That is, all non-Jewish nations will be blessed. The genealogy of Abraham's offspring that opens the New Testament is therefore a substantive reminder of the promise that is about to be fulfilled in the events that immediately follow, that according to the Abrahamic covenant will be for all nations, not just the Jewish people. Furthermore, as Paul argues in Romans 4, Abraham is the father in the faith of "all of us" who believe (4:16). Two other references seem to amplify and confirm this, except on closer study, only one in fact does so. When the angel of the Lord tells the shepherds that this "good news of great joy" is going to be "for *all the people*" (Luke 2:10) the word used for people is *laos* which would have been understood as referring to the people of Israel, not all people generally. The second reference however is specific. Simeon takes Jesus in his arms and prophesies that He will be "a light for revelation to the Gentiles" (Luke 3:32). However, the fact is that references to the Jews as the beneficiaries of this birth far outrun those to Gentiles.

The beginning of the gospel story by Matthew and Luke that accounts for the "good news" that comes in the birth of Christ, is paralleled in Paul's seminal exposition of that gospel in his letter to the Romans, where he repeats who this gospel was for. In his opening chapter, he affirms the emphasis of the incarnation story, that the gospel is "for the salvation of *everyone* who believes" but it is *"first for the Jew"* (Romans 1:16). The Greek word used here (*proton*) means 'first' both in particularity but also in prominence. This is the most ignored truth of the incarnation narrative, and arguably the most neglected matter for public acknowledgement in Gentile Advent homilies and services. Sadly, there are reasons for this, some of them arising from a supercessionist theology (or what we term 'replacement theology').

The birth narratives tell us that the Messiah came as a Jew to the Jewish people. "From the Jews is traced the human ancestry of Christ" (Romans 9:5). Questions about this Jewish priority, this overture theme of "to the Jew first", are answered by scripture in so many ways.

- The Jews are God's self-described chosen people (Deuteronomy 7:6; Romans 11: 28-29).
- Jesus Himself said, "salvation is from the Jews" (John 4:22). He commissioned His disciples to first go to "the lost sheep of the house of Israel" (Matthew 10:5-6).
- As Paul expressed it, the advantage in being a Jew was that "first of all, they have been entrusted with the very words of God" (Romans 3:2).
- They were the first to be evangelized: "We had to speak the Word of God to you first." It is at this point that Paul then says, "We now turn to the Gentiles" (Acts 13:46).
- The blessing of "glory, honor and peace for everyone who does good" is "first for the Jew, then for the Gentile" (Romans 2:10). What qualifies any possible Gentile resentment is that "trouble and distress for every human being who does evil" is also "first for the Jew" (2:9). God "does not show favoritism" (2:11).

Two equal and opposite problems result from an unbiblical view of this 'Jewish priority'. This has often been presented as the result of a failure to understand our true worth to Christ:

- *"I wish I was Jewish."* This is a 'wannabee' Gentile mentality that expresses a deflated sense of self-worth, unknowing of Paul's explanation that "in Christ Jesus" Gentiles are now no longer "aliens to the *commonwealth of Israel*" and no longer "strangers to the *covenants of promise*" (Ephesians 2:12).
- *"I am the new Jew."* This is premised on a belief that the church has replaced Israel, and is the new Israel. This is not just 'replacement' but 'displacement' theology. This is expressing an inflated sense of self-worth. Paul's response to this is unequivocal: "Do not be arrogant" (Romans 11:20).

Two truths must be held together that are complementary and not contradictory. The incarnation is the story of salvation coming to everyone, but coming to the Jews first. This should produce many powerful responses and effects at Advent in the lives of those of us who are Gentile Christians.

- For all our affections of joy at Advent, we should be able to relate also to the "great sorrow and unceasing anguish" of Paul's heart, as he acknowledges so many reasons for the priority of the gospel's call to the Jewish people: "Theirs is the adoption as sons; theirs the divine glory, the covenants, the receiving of the law, the temple worship and the promises. Theirs are the patriarchs, and from them is traced the human ancestry of Christ" (Romans 9: 4-5). Yet they are absent at our celebration of Yeshua HaMashiach's birth (Romans 9:2).

- This affection should then be expressed in our Advent prayers and not omitted from our liturgies: "My heart's desire and prayer to God for the Israelites is that they may be saved" (Romans 10:1).

- The humility we experience at Advent is primarily provoked by the example of Jesus who "humbled Himself" by taking on "human likeness" (Philippians 2:7). But the Gentile admission that the gospel was to the Jew first should provoke a Gentile confession of such humble gratitude that Gentiles "have received mercy as a result of their disobedience". But this mercy that we have received through the Messiah's coming is "that they too may now receive mercy" as a result of God's mercy to Gentiles. This provides another opportunity for humility. As Paul put it, "salvation has come to the Gentiles to make Israel envious" (Romans 11:11). Paul warns us: "Do not boast ... If you do, consider this: You do not support the root, but the root supports you." Humility is an Advent disposition. Perhaps the tree we should choose at Christmas is the Olive Tree, just to remind us at Advent of the "kindness" of God to us, who though "wild by nature" were grafted into "their (the Jewish) olive tree" (Romans 11:11-24).

Advent should put the need for Jewish people to know their Messiah, Yeshua, back on our spiritual map. The Jewish priority that is presented by the gospel writers should provoke both our Advent prayers as well as our Advent praise. There is no priority in righteousness for there are none who are righteous, neither Jew nor Gentile. We therefore come to the Messiah's manger equally dependent on God's mercy and grace. Ethnic affiliation does not give superior seating or private viewing. "Is God the God of the

Jews only? Is He not the God of the Gentiles too? Yes, of Gentiles too, since there is only one God who will justify the circumcised by faith and the uncircumcised through that same faith" (Romans 3:29-30). This Advent, do not forget to thank God that both the Jewish shepherds and the Gentile wise men had equally supernatural invitations to the same Christ in the same crib, to the same Yeshua in the same barn. And so do you, regardless of tribe, or people or nation. What a gathering of Jews and Gentiles it is going to be at the second Advent, that the first one, the overture, makes us long for with deepening expectation.

Treetorial

"They set up sacred stones ... under every spreading tree."
(2 Kings 17:10)

While choirs exhort me to rejoice,
I'm numbed and needled by a choice
I have to make, immediately,
The purchase of a Christmas tree.
What chance my family will concur
That I selected the right fir?
Would it be deemed heretical
If it were not symmetrical?
Which Douglas, Balsam, Fraser or
Nordman would fit through my front door?
Competing features call a truce.
Perhaps I should check out a spruce.
Perhaps a Serbian would do,
Or maybe Colorado Blue.
If all these options I decline,
There's Scottish or Virginia pine.
The indecision breeds duress.
Would a Cypress relieve the stress?

But wait, they say our Christmas tree
Came from Gentile idolatry;
That evergreens served to appease
Saturn the god of wealth and peace.

I could use this as my excuse
For shunning Fir, resisting Spruce.
Self-righteously I could decline
The soft Cypress, the fragrant Pine.
So why do Gentile symbols reign,
If Christ was born in Jews' domain?
When the angelic gospel burst,
Was it not proclaimed to Jews first?
And are not Gentiles neither root,
Nor even a natural shoot?
Did we not travel in the aft,
And were we not a gracious graft?
Why, yes indeed, thus now I see,
The Olive is my Christmas tree.

"You were grafted into a cultivated olive tree."
(Romans 11:24)
(2017)

Stumped

It is impossible to engage the Advent season without encountering the subject of hope. The New Testament is 'new' precisely because it is a new day of hope after 400 years of hopeless silence and nearly two thousand years of unfulfilled hoping for a promised Messiah. The entire Old Testament from Genesis 3:15 onwards (when the "seed of woman" was predicted to bruise the serpent's head) records and reveals the Messianic Hope – the longing for the Messiah, the anointed one, the deliverer and the redeemer. As teachers through the ages have pointed out, it is not enough to even say that the Old Testament contains prophecies. It has been argued that it is a prophecy from first to last and embodies the progressive revelation of an incredible hope. As you turn the pages of the Bible, one covenant follows another: with Adam, with Noah, with Abraham, with Moses, and with David. Revelation is given about the hope that is to be realized in the coming of the Messiah, or in Greek, the Christ. Jesus would one day say of Abraham that he "rejoiced to see my day: and he saw it and was glad" (John 8:56).

The Advent story is the celebration of this hope fulfilled: it is indeed about hope for the hopeless. Not surprisingly, the music and hymnody that celebrates the incarnation is specific about this hope:

> Hark, the glad sound! The Savior comes,
> *The Savior promised long;*
> Let every heart prepare a throne,
> And every voice a song.

In the well-loved carol, "O little town of Bethlehem", we sing that the "hopes ... of all the years are met in thee tonight." Matthew (2:4-6) quotes

Micah (5:2) on this: "But you Bethlehem, in the land of Judah, are by no means least among the rulers of Judah; **for out of you will come a ruler** who will be the shepherd of my people Israel." In 1744 Charles Wesley wrote his hymn "Come Thou Long-Expected Jesus," and it reads:

Come, Thou *long-expected Jesus,*
Born to set Thy people free;
From our fears and sins release us;
Let us find our rest in Thee.
Israel's strength and consolation,
Hope of all the earth Thou art;
Dear desire of every nation,
Joy of every *longing* heart.

It is Jesus Himself who is our authority for understanding that the Old Testament scriptures were the messages of hope for His coming: "Search the scriptures ... and they are they which testify of me" (John 5:39). "Beginning with Moses and with all the prophets, He explained to them what was said in all the scriptures concerning Himself" (Luke 24:27). We get a good idea of the passages that Jesus referred to by listening to the ones that the apostles used to acknowledge and affirm who Jesus is as our hope. A passage like Psalm 110 is used more than any other. Jesus would have given them this exposition in those 40 days of post-resurrection scriptural study. He gave them a thorough overview of the way that the different divisions of scripture (Law, Prophets, including the Historical books, and devotional writings) all presented the pre-incarnate Christ, the pre-figuring of His Messiahship.

What is arguably the best-known gospel verse? Most people would say John 3:16. But what precedes it? "And as Moses lifted up the serpent in the wilderness, even so must the Son of Man be lifted up: that whosoever believes in Him should not perish." What sign did Jesus say would be given the evil and adulterous generation? He said it was "the sign of Jonah. For as Jonas was three days and three nights in the whale's belly, so shall the Son of Man be three days and three nights in the heart of the earth" (Matthew 12:39-40). Do you remember Paul talking of the institutions and ordinances of Jewish faith as "a shadow of things that were to come" (Colossians 2:17)? In Jesus' coming, longing came out of the shadows, the meaning of the signs was realized, hope expected became hope experienced, and hope conceived became hope completed.

Some of the most dramatic evidence that the Bible is a supernatural book and not a collection of stories and myths is the unavoidable proof of fulfilled messianic prophecy. It has been estimated that there are some 2500 prophecies in the Bible, almost 2000 of which have been fulfilled to the letter. It has been estimated that there are 333 prophecies in the Old Testament that were fulfilled in the Messiah. Devout Jews prayed earnestly for the day when He would arrive. Simeon, in the Lucan account of the incarnation, is a wonderful example of this; a man of faith who was "looking for the consolation of Israel" (Luke 2:25). When he saw Jesus as an infant, Simeon knew that this child was the fulfillment of his messianic hope. Charles Wesley was borrowing from this passage when he described Jesus in his hymn as "Israel's strength and consolation."

But although Jesus fulfilled all these prophecies for Israel's Messiah, He came to bring salvation to the entire world, which is what Wesley was referring to when he described Christ as the "hope of *all the earth*" and the "dear desire of every nation". He is the "joy of *every longing heart*". Here is one well-known presentation of this prefiguring hope.

Messiah (Christ) In The Old Testament

- In Genesis He is the Seed of the woman (3:15).
- In Exodus He is the Lamb of God for sinners slain (12:5-7,11).
- In Leviticus He is our High Priest (the whole book).
- In Numbers He is the Star out of Jacob (24:17).
- In Deuteronomy He is the Prophet like unto Moses (18:15).
- In Joshua He is the Captain of the Lord's armies (5:13-15).
- In Judges He is the Angel of the LORD or the messenger of Jehovah (13:18-23).
- In Ruth He is our Kinsman-Redeemer (Chapter 3).
- In Samuel, Kings and Chronicles He is the King of Kings and Lord of Lords (1 Samuel 8:2-9).
- In Ezra, Nehemiah and Esther He is the sovereign Lord over all the kingdoms of the earth (entire books).

- In Job He is our risen and returning Redeemer (19:25).
- In Psalms He is the Blessed Man (1), Son of Man (2), Crucified One (22), Coming One (24), Reigning One (72).
- In Proverbs He is our Wisdom (14).
- In Ecclesiastes He is the forgotten Wise Man (9:14-15).
- In Song of Solomon He is my Beloved (2:16).
- In Isaiah He is our suffering Substitute (53).
- In Jeremiah He is the Lord Our Righteousness (23:6).
- In Lamentations He is the Man of sorrows who weeps for His people (1:12-18).
- In Ezekiel He is the glory of God (1:28).
- In Daniel He is the Smiting Stone (2:34) and the Companion in the furnace of fire and the den of lions (3:24-25, 6:22).
- In Hosea He is David's Greater King (3:5).
- In Joel He is the Hope of His people (3:16).
- In Amos He is the Rescuer of Israel (3:12).
- In Obadiah He is the Deliverer upon Mount Zion (1:17).
- In Jonah He is the buried and risen Savior (compare Matthew 12:40).
- In Micah He is the Everlasting God born in Bethlehem (5:2).
- In Nahum He is our Stronghold in the day of wrath (1:7).
- In Habakkuk He is the Anchor of our faith (2:4).
- In Zephaniah He is in the midst for judgment and cleansing (3:5,15).
- In Haggai He is Lord of presence and power (1:13).
- In Zechariah He is the smitten Shepherd (13:7).
- In Malachi He is the Sun of Righteousness (4:2).

The entire Old Testament bears testimony to the hope and expectation of a Savior, the one who will be great to the ends of the earth. This hope is continuously and constantly captured in the declaration that "He comes!"

But as true and insistent, and as powerful and inevitable as this onward movement of messianic hope happens to be, there is yet another reality. There is equally a true and realistic presentation of the sin and sadness, the fear and failure, the rejection and ruin, the desertion and denial, the rebellion and resistance, the abandonment and adultery, the idolatry and immorality, the desecration and defilement that called into question this hope by virtue of the sheer consequential hopelessness that overcame both individual and nation. We learn so much about this from the prophets, but it is precisely because of their understanding and revelation of the hope that they were able to walk through the darkness in a way that was triumphant and true.

There is no better example of this than Isaiah, whose prophecies get so much airtime during Advent. In chapter 6, the last few verses describe the hopelessness: cities ruined, houses deserted, fields ravaged, the land forsaken and wasted. Thank God for that "but" in v13. The forest of their pride has been burned down; they have been reduced by circumstance and the greenery of their apparent health has been reduced to ashes. "*But* as the terebinth and oak leave stumps when they are cut down, so the holy seed will be the stump in the land" (6:13). In a landscape of hopelessness, there is yet a stump. That stump revives the memory of Job, who in his hopelessness uses the same image: "At least there is hope for a tree: if it is cut down it will sprout again, and its new shoots will not fail. Its roots may grow old in the ground and its stump die in the soil, yet at the scent of water it will bud and put forth shoots like a plant" (14:7). A stump of spiritual hope with God is better than a forest of fleshly hope without Him. When the world seemed to be cloaked in doom, hope was always the fringe of the garment. The infrastructures of personal life and nation were collapsing but the promised hope of the Messiah is given: the "holy seed." It is indeed edgy precisely because it is life on the ledge. Suddenly, Isaiah's recovered hope becomes a precedent for trusting God for the nation.

Isaiah cannot keep this godly hope down. "The Lord himself will give you a sign: the virgin will be with child and will give birth to a son and will call him Immanuel" (7:14). But despite the continuing evidences of hopelessness resulting from continuing sin, God gives the characteristics of a remnant that will choose against the odds to hope in God (8:12). They are marked by a different orientation of life, a different outlook, a different authority (the Word) and consequently a different view of the future. Then comes chapter 9, all written in the past tense as if what it describes has already happened, even though none of it has yet taken place. Because of Isaiah's hope in the love of God and the Word of the Lord, he can talk about it as the reality it is; he can see the light at the end of the tunnel, even though present experience is bleak and black. He sees that God will honor "the Galilee of the Gentiles." Did not the child grow up to be known as "Jesus of Galilee"? Chapter 10 continues the promise that the yoke will be broken and lifted from the people's neck by a deliverer, and again (v33) the forests of men's pride and strength will be felled. The vision of hopelessness makes way for a second presentation of glorious hope: "A shoot will come up from the stump of Jesse. From his roots a Branch will bear fruit" (11:1). Here is the process of the messianic hope: a stump, a root, a branch, and fruit. But right now, hope is stumped.

And that is how the New Testament begins, with a nation and a couple whose hopes are stumped. The narrative of hopelessness with which the Old Testament ended seemed to be continuing unabated. Remember that the last word in the Old Testament was "curse". The people's hopelessness is systemic. They were worn down by years of disappointment and the shame that went with it. Hopelessness breeds shame. Now you know why scripture says that God's hope does not disappoint us and does not make us ashamed

The New Testament begins with a stump, and with people who are stumped. But it is that root from the stump of Jesse that breaks through in the birth of Jesus and that brings the shoots to every other stump. The Advent message of the gospel is that the redeeming and healing power of Christ is still in the business of restoring stumps, especially stumped hopes. This Advent, let us ask the Holy Spirit to be and to do what Paul describes in Romans 5:5: "Hope does not disappoint us because God has poured out His love into our hearts by the Holy Spirit." In the light of this coming, this fulfillment of messianic hope, there is no reason for any disappointment that would rob us of the blessed hope, not only for life now, but also for that which is yet to come, the Second Advent no less. The incarnation announces the glorious news that there is no need to live a stumped life any longer. Just as Isaiah foresaw it, the spirit of heaviness from stumped hopes, was going to be replaced by a garment of praise, when those stumps became the "trees of righteousness, the planting of the Lord."

Nativity: Of Christ, Of Nicodemus, Of Me

"You must be born again. The wind blows wherever it pleases."
(John 3: 7-8)

Like wrinkled leaves of withered, veined, browned fall-down hope,
They were firm rustled from afar
And near, gust-gathered shepherd lads,
Spirit-swept, wind-winnowed magi,
Blown like longing spores upon
The currents of eternal will
Until their searching scurried
In through stabled doors to settle still
And green again around the root of Jesse's stump.

Thus was the story whispered in Sanhedrin halls.
It roused his brittle soul to ask,
Does that wind yet blow where it wills?
Then draught-drawn, this frail Pharisee,
One dank-dusked and autumnal night,
Though aged and weathered by the law,
Was soft-seized by a gale of Grace
That left him crumpled-clean and free,
Quite born again, around the shoot of Jesse's stump.

I have heard, Nicodemus, these same childbirth cries,
As my eyes raked through gospel leaves,
Until a midwife-voice did speak
To me of my nativity.
"The spirit does the Spirit
Birth, and wind blows where it pleases."
Yes, I did ask like you, "How can
This be?" Then, "Let it be!" I cried.
I was delivered at the foot of Jesse's stump.

"Jesus answered ... the Spirit gives birth to spirit."
(John 3:6)
(2013)

A Stitch In Time

The birth narratives are full of brilliantly broad brush-strokes of divine activity, but there are also bristles of exquisite revelation. In this barn, full of grainy truth, can we find a helpful needle in a haystack, a graspable point amidst hundreds of stalks of prophetic fulfillment? In the Lucan account there is a single word, that like a deft needle in the hand of a skilled seamstress, enters and re-emerges in the fabric of the plot, indelibly stitching the creative purpose of the artist into the tapestry of history. Follow this needle as it pulls the thread of Creator God's intent: "Elizabeth said, 'In these days He has shown His *favor* ... Greetings, you who are highly *favored* ... The angel said to her, 'Do not be afraid, Mary, you have found *favor* with God ... Why am I so *favored* that the mother of my Lord should come to me? ... Suddenly a great company of the heavenly host appeared with the angel, praising God and saying, 'Glory to God in the highest, and on earth peace to men on whom His *favor* rests' ... and Jesus grew in *favor* with God and men ... The people were amazed at the words of *favor* that came from His lips ... to proclaim the year of the Lord's favor" (Luke 1:25, 28, 30, 43; 2:14, 52; 4:22; Isaiah 61:2)

From Elizabeth's miraculous conception to Mary's immaculate one, from the Judean shepherds' private angelic concert to the emergence of Jesus in public ministry, the flashing of the divine purpose, and the fusing of the divine plot are all captured in the pin-point prick of gleaming, glinting grace. So far, so good, but actually it had not felt good for a very long time. Everything seemed far from favorable. All was fragile perhaps, and certainly fearful, but definitely not favorable.

Lest we think that all this favor is predictably divine for a birth like this, and consequently sentimentalize, minimize and trivialize what this actually means, we should consider the realities of the situation into which this word was embroidered and observe the national, political, social, moral, personal, spiritual context that prevailed. This favor did not exist in a vacuum. As always it seems, grace found grief, as favor found fear. We are well versed in the story but should not allow familiarity to ignore the details.

"He was chosen by lot according to the custom" (Luke 1:9).

Of course this was meant to be an honor for Zechariah. There was one chance in 18,000 that your name would be drawn out of the hat. Yes, it was special, but there was no reason to expect anything unusual that would cause the incense-pot to be dropped. After all, national religion had been going through a quiet phase for the last four hundred years. It seemed like the endless re-run of some old movies, like *Captive in Egypt* and *Exiled in Babylon.* And they were of the silent kind. If God had been dumb for so long then there was no fear of Him speaking this year. If He was deaf, then why should there be any expectation of an answer to yet another ritualistic rendition of the priestly liturgical prayer that pleaded for the redemption of Israel? If you are Zechariah, God was as wordless as his wife was childless. Have a nice service. This was duty not delight. It was like dressing up for a party where not only does the host forget to order the food and wine, and the chairs and tables, but actually forgets to show up himself. Favor was not on the menu.

"Many of the people of Israel will be brought back" (Luke 1:16).

"Will be" sounds good but what about now? It would be great but these words of Gabriel to Zechariah remind us that the present situation was dominated by national backsliding, by spiritual decline, by Spiritless religion. Favor was not in the land.

"Turn the hearts of the fathers to the children and the
disobedient to the wisdom of the righteous" (Luke 1:17).

Every promise, every prophetic announcement, infers the pains and the problems that explained why mercy would indeed need to be "tender". Not only were the times out of sync but also the generations were disconnected and the rank and file were living in daily disobedience to the Word of God. Favor was not in the family.

"To make a people prepared" (Luke 1:17).

Unpreparedness was the order of the day, born out of hearts that had ceased to believe, to expect, to anticipate, or to hope. It was like a 'once-upon-a-time' romance that had degenerated into repetition, and a repetition that had festered into rejection. The couple that was suddenly on-stage and under the spotlight, Elizabeth and Zechariah, was representative of all the national fathers and mothers, all the people who had learned to live with no expectation for change. Favor was not in the future.

"When he came out he could not speak" (Luke 1:22).

There was no shortage of cultural cynicism. Dark Jewish humor was having a heyday. The people had been waiting patiently outside for this longer-than-usual liturgy. Was the routine so dull that the priest had fallen asleep mid-prayer? Had he died? That would be symbolic of the death of public faith. Fortunately, he had not. "They realized he had seen a vision in the temple" (Luke 1:22). Was the incense hallucinogenic? If you really wanted to believe that something had just transpired that was not only extraordinary, but something uncharacteristically good, then would it not be just depressively "typical" that Zechariah could not tell them about it? Did they feel the cat was playing with the mouse? What was the takeaway as the worshipers trooped home, partially animated by something clearly unusual, but essentially none the wiser for it. As if things were not bleak or bad enough at this point in the story, the silence of four centuries was going to continue to live on in Zechariah's mouth. Favor was not in his mouth. Happy Advent!

We have only experienced Scene One of Luke's drama, and already we have a clear picture of the depression, disappointment, delay, despair, joyless dutifulness, and dead dreams that characterized the terrain of the heart, the home and the homeland. Where was the favor? Consider the takeaway of the frustrated worshipers, who left to face another year of unanswered prayers. Is there any takeaway for the reader? Are we left just to identify with the suffering and the silence? Is there any help for our equal experience of national darkness and lostness? The redeeming feature of the liturgy here was that despite no answers to the annual intercessions, at least it kept them committed to pray, long after their spontaneous and informal prayers had succumbed to dumbness. The encouragement to endure and persevere in prayer against the odds, into the wind, against the current, seems to be regarded as integral to everything that took place in this story, according to Anna's experience anyway. And let us not miss the fact that the initial breakthrough revelation from heaven in the form of Gabriel was at the place of prayer. Surely that was an endorsement of heaven for the rugged obedience to ask and keep on asking, despite feeling ragged, and even miserably religious because everything felt more by rote than by faith.

At this point in the story, we have the advantage over the worshipers who were in the outside court, simply because the story puts us on the inside with Zechariah. We hear what he hears. The first words from heaven after those eons of silence were astoundingly unexpected: "Your prayer has been heard" (Luke 1:13). We do not know exactly, whenever we begin to pray, when our asking for this or that request will be completed because it has been satisfactorily answered. Like Israel, it is easy to forget what Isaiah had said: "For Zion's sake I will not keep silent … I will not keep quiet UNTIL …" (Isaiah 62:1). Until? Until when? Of course "until" feels too open-ended, especially when years roll by and we are tempted to wonder if God's ears are closed and heaven too is closed for further business.

It is interesting that the very first word from heaven through Gabriel about "the spirit and power of Elijah" exactly repeats the prophetic promise of the very last words of the Old Testament, when the Lord says through Malachi: "I will send you the prophet Elijah before that great and dreadful day of the Lord comes" (Malachi 4:5). Although it seemed to us that there was a breakdown in communication with heaven, it turns out that there was no break at all, as Gabriel picks up where Malachi left off, repeating the very same promise. What we must learn from this moment in Israel's prayer history is wrapped up in Malachi's use of the word "before". Was not the coming of Elijah the answer they were then waiting for? Was this not the promise fulfilled and the prayer answered? Indeed, Zechariah's boy was coming "in the spirit and power of Elijah" but if this was the "before" then there must be an "after."

What Zechariah may have thought was the final answer, turned out to be the preface and prelude to something else. To what? Did not Malachi say it was the "dreadful" day of the Lord, not the "wonderful" one? The meaning of "the day of the Lord" was a two-sided coin for Israel that became a euphemism more for judgment than for favor. Regardless, it was understood that it would be a theophany, a visible manifestation of God to man. It was just expected to be fearful not favorable. Yes, John was indeed an answer to prayer, "before" the day of the Lord, but Gabriel goes on to refer to John as going "before the Lord" Himself. The fruits of John's ministry (turning the hearts of the fathers to the children and turning the disobedient to the wisdom of the righteous) are intimating something wonderful not dreadful, favorable not fearful. The needle of grace is emerging again and after four hundred years favor is being embroidered in the fabric of personal and national life.

This Advent, the story about Zechariah's prayer for a baby can speak to all of our unanswered prayer lists, with the reminder that in His answering, God is not simply relating to our need, but relating our answer to any other number of His loving and gracious purposes. While we want favor for ourselves alone, or for our nation alone, God wants His gracious salvation for everyone, everywhere, forever. While we are dominated in our asking by the immediate exigencies of our temporal situation, God is thinking "eternal". After years and years, Zechariah had given up on asking for a baby. He had just wanted a child but through the child, God wanted the messenger that Malachi prophesied about, and beyond him, He wanted the Messiah, His "One and Only" to be born. The stitch of favor that was John, was the foreword for the Word that "became flesh and made His dwelling among us ... the glory of the One and Only who came from the Father, full of grace and truth" (John 1:14). This was the day of the Lord indeed. This was a theophany of favor not fear. The answer that we eventually receive as the conclusion of our asking is but God's means for His continuing answers. Through the answer to Zechariah's prayers, He was not only able to fill their small crib but also fill the nations with His grace and glory.

So where did that needle of favor go? It stitched the message that the worst of human times are always still a time of grace. As the prophet Zechariah reminded us, the Holy Spirit, in the worst of days, at the end of time, is a "spirit of supplication", but thank God, also a "spirit of grace" (Zechariah 12:7). There is grace in the asking for those who ask for it. As one imprisoned Soviet saint put it at a time of great national darkness: "the train of God's grace is always on time." He did not live to experience the release from his prison that he prayed for, but he arrived at heaven's terminus, exactly on time. Meanwhile, a stitch of grace in time saves … way more than nine.

Dragon, Behold the Lamb

"The great dragon was hurled down."
(Revelation 12:9)

Our days were carrion-clawed to death.
The talon-ravaged nights would breed,
And each delivered stillborn deed
Was midwifed by the dragon's breath.
Damp silence like hoarfrost fell,
As Satan's soldiery caroused.
No citizen could be aroused,
Though rapiered by the morning's bell.
The reptile played the sovereign's part,
And cast his shedding scales on all,
Which like confetti'd hate would fall
And cling to every human heart.
His cohorts loved to mouth and mock.
While they sucked pig and swilled the beast,
The dragon ordered for his feast
A lamb, the choicest of the flock.

Shepherds were wearying of the night,
When clarioned-majesty broke through
Their dark, and wide-winged flew
In choreographic grace and light.
The choral acclamation told
Of age's mystery unveiled,
And of a lamb that would be hailed

As the perfection of the fold.
The dragon heard and laughing, leered;
That lamb once found would be his fare.
He over-spilled his scalding lair,
And Rachel's weeping heart was seared.
At last upon a butcher's block,
Pure innocence was shaved and shorn.
The dragon's meat was red-toothed torn,
A lamb, the choicest of the flock.

The hounds of Hades bayed no more;
The sated spirits slumped and slept.
Three days had passed since satyrs kept
A watchful eye upon the door.
A trumpet blew, horn of a ram,
It shook the earth and raised the dead,
And every spirit woke in dread,
Out of Gehenna walked a lamb.
The demons tried to hide and cower,
For in His hands they saw the claws,
The fangs, the teeth of dragon-jaws;
Plucked by the roots was Sheol's power.
The lamb looked like it had been slain.
Before him shorn wolves rushed headlong;
Behind him burst a shepherd's song
As myriads voiced the new refrain:
"Worthy, worthy is the Lamb,
On the dragon's head He trod;
Worthy, worthy is the Lamb,
Choicest of the flock of God."

"They will make war against the Lamb, but the Lamb will triumph."
(Revelation 17:14)

(1987)

Dumb and Dumber

Zechariah was no spiritual novice. He was a mature priest and he was pious. He is described as "blameless" but piety did not give immunity from pain. No doubt this honor of performing a week of service with its auspicious responsibilities served his desire to finish his ministry well. He had spiritual experience but perhaps in his aging he had got long in the spiritual tooth and frankly could have done with a fresh encounter with God to see him through to the end. Was he inwardly hoping for that as he made his way through the countryside? Was there any uplift of longing as he saw the Temple come into view? Was there an explanation for why he was not quite as straight-shouldered as he used to be? Did he think about the shared burden with his wife when he was greeted and honored by the young men who he passed on the road, sons of blessed fathers? He and Elizabeth were indeed "well-along in years" and he was feeling them as he started the climb towards the City. They had struggled to accept that their family tree, and therefore their family future, was as sapless, leafless and lifeless as the truncated stump of Jesse. Their barrenness was symbolic of the times, and a microcosm of national hopelessness and helplessness. Despite every attempt to do the right thing, whether characterized by another perfumed attempt at private lovemaking or another incense-clouded priestly prayer in public, nothing was happening. Seed was continually sown but there was no fertilization, whether in Elizabeth's womb or in the soil of messianic history. Where was that harvest of justice and joy that the prophets spoke about? This felt more like the Negev of deserted comfort.

So he won the lottery. Maybe he was not as lost in heaven's bureaucracy as he had come to believe. But he still thought his prayers were lost in transmission. As he prepared to begin the liturgy, it occurred to him that despite the times being out of joint, it perhaps felt easier to pray and believe for the nation than for his own needs. Although he began the prayers, it was another voice than Zechariah's that said "Amen." The theology of answered prayer had taken a beating for generations now, so one can empathize with Zechariah's numbness at the angelic appearance. As we have noted, the national issues dominated Zechariah's public prayer as a priest in the Temple. However, it was his wife Elizabeth's barrenness that had burdened his private supplications as a husband. So when Gabriel said, "Your prayer is heard," was Zechariah's startled surprise at the visitation augmented by a painful perplexity about what on earth was meant? "*My prayer?*" Which one? Was it the priestly prayer for the redemption of Israel ... "You will have a son" ... or the one that Elizabeth and I have been praying for years ... "and he will be great in the sight of the Lord." He could be forgiven for not understanding that this announcement provided the connection between the two prayers. Have we not already agreed that our greatest longings only make ultimate sense and are only truly realized when they find their meaning, not simply as the outcome of our narrow and domestic desires, but as the fulfillment of God's global and eternal purposes? And would he be the first to wonder why the One who was omniscient seemed to be carrying on without a serious bit of information?

But I'm old ... "And he will make ready a people prepared for the Lord" ... and what's worse, so is the wife ... but thanks for the thought. To put it bluntly, she is barren and I am bald and her hair is thinning now as well, come to think of it. Zechariah's response at the beginning of this new revelation to Israel was a bit like Abraham's at the beginning of the original version. The record shows that Abraham laughed at the promise long before Sarah did (Genesis 17:17; 18:12). God is hardly tapping into a faith-gusher. Here is an incredible supernatural revelation after four hundred years, an angelic visit and the promise of the miracle that he has always wanted more than anything else. He is in the holy place with all of its awesome significance and he seems to be arguing, if not playing hard to get. Do you catch the tremor of a 'read-my-lips-buddy' kind of tone in Gabriel's voice as he is forced to present his credentials? Speaking succinctly and slowly: "I am Gabriel (not just Angel Tom, or Angel Dick or Angel Harry) and I stand in the Presence of God (permanently, in the center of divine operations, in the hearing of the throne, not in some basement office waiting for a memo) and I have been sent to speak to you (though why you beats me - you cannot be the right guy) and to tell you the good news (and I mean good on God's terms but would you know good news if you heard it anyway?)" It is an ironic twist. God is silent and the priest talks. God speaks and the priest is dumb.

Even in those days, people were fascinated by the way robed priests moved, as if they were floating and gliding over the ground, unlike mere mortals who got dirt between their toes. Zechariah definitely did not have his hovering gear engaged when he emerged from the holy place. He did not seem to be worried about the angle of his turban or his sash. His arms were flailing, and it was not clear what he was trying to either sign or mime. The contrast between such a pristine clear communication from heaven and the incoherence of his evangelistic semaphores just added to the frustration and pain.

"You will be silent and unable to speak." Be honest. Have you ever thought that this was a tad severe, just as you have thought that Esau seemed to get a hard rap, all for a bowl of stew? You must understand that it was not about Esau's choice of meat. By treating as valueless the birthright and the blessing, he had treated the covenant, the summation of God's love and grace, as irrelevant, and that irrelevance was irreverence. It was a terrible sin against God's character and against relationship. The reason for Zechariah's punishment was given: "because you did not believe my words" (Luke 1:20). In refusing belief for his present circumstances he was denying God's work for the needs of the world. That too was a sin against God's character and against covenant relationship. Is it not amazing how flippantly we excuse our intermittent atheism? We shrug our shoulders self-excusingly and without any conviction we say, "I just didn't believe it" and then carry on without batting an eyelid. God takes unbelief personally.

Zechariah would not be the first or the last to experience this dumbness. Our mouths are silenced by one of two things: fear or unbelief. Consequently, we fail to make a good confession. The Greek word for confession is *homologeo* that is made up of two words meaning 'same word' or speaking the same thing. To cease to confess is simply to stop saying the same things about life and reality that God is saying. When Zechariah chose not to accept God's Word but doubt it, when he chose not to speak **with** God, then he lost the ability to speak **for** God. We may not have been struck physically dumb, but spiritual dumbness is a crippling condition when our worship before heaven and our witness before the world are silenced. In scripture, silence was most often a judgment against falsehood and arrogance. For Zechariah not to accept the truth of Gabriel's news was both of these: holding on to the falsehood that God was unable to do what He said, and pride in his doubt being the final word on the matter. Yes, there was judgment here, but I believe there was more grace as Zechariah was going to be forced into a place with God, to recover submission, trust and belief. The chastising was the discipline of God. Through this judgment he was going to recover His joy. The silencing of his own words was going to help him listen to God's Word. He was going to recover his spiritual hearing through his dumbness, so that when he did speak again, he would say what God was saying.

How does this advent find us? Has any unbelief or any fear imposed an ungodly silence on us? Has any accusation or condemnation silenced our confidence in asking of God? Do we find ourselves at a place where our life is not aligned with God's Word, where our thoughts about things are not His thoughts? In Zechariah's recovery of his speech there are clues for our own healing and deliverance. How on earth did he finish out that week of service? And when he got home, did he initiate the lovemaking by any chance? I wonder.

Beget, Begat, Begot

"... Of whom was born Jesus who is called the Christ ..."
(Matthew 1:16)

Beget, begat, begot. I neither love nor read the script
Of unknown dead.
Those genealogies, like some long-attic'd sepia'd spool
Time-scratched and grained,
Strange names unloop in flash-print spasms of short-shallow breath,
And in a blink,
Without memoriam from those begat, they now beget
Amnesia.
First Adam did beget a son of first creation, Cain,
Sin on the run,
And Abram did beget a covenant's long-promised son,
Sign on the rocks.
Whoever begat so-and-so, who begat what's-his-name.
Begotten then forgotten.

Beget, begat, begot. How can the Testament that's new
Begin like this?
And Eleazar begat Matthan who Jacob begets
Who begat not
Your ordinary Joe who begets ... begat ... begot ... who?
That spool unreels.
The generational dull metronome, that beats life's death,
Explodes apart,
Unable to process the interruptive mention of

A woman's name.
Thus with one word, Mary, God felled the family tree of man's
Fallen descent
Of whom was begot Jesus, the one who is called the Christ.
Begotten yet forgotten.

Beget, begat, begot. How I now love to read that script,
Of born again.
That stem from Jesse's root has now grown my familial tree,
My fruitful branch
That genealogy of Jesus Christ that records all
Who were begat
Of God, begotten not of natural descent, begat
Not of a man's
Decision nor of husband's choice, but of the Father's will.
And God begat
Both you and me. Now I wish none would skip the page and miss
That I am there,
And all the progeny that through the gospel He'll beget.
Begotten not forgotten.

> *"Yet to all who received Him, to those who believed*
> *in His name, He gave the right to become*
> *children of God."*
> (John 1:13)
> (2014)

Talking of Silence

After Malachi, the last prophet of the Old Testament, there was a long silence that only speaks of how dark and deep the loss of relationship with God had become. There are few of us who do not know the kind of silence that speaks loudly of a rift in relationship, a lessening and loosening of love-talk. In the prophets, silence is a sign of judgment: "I have put an end to the shouting" (Isaiah 16:10). In the Psalms, silence is the evidence of things being out of sync and disturbed: "I am so troubled that I cannot speak." We all know that kind of wordlessness and speechlessness that grips us in silence. We talk about being dumb-founded, do we not?

If silence is the great motif, the unsettling manifestation of a broken relationship with God, represented by a single white, blank, wordless dividing sheet in our Bibles between Malachi and Matthew, then the recovery of sound becomes the great image of renewed intimacy and joy. I do not think it is without significance that the Lucan narrative begins the whole story with what happened to Zechariah. Four hundred years of heaven's silence is suddenly, dramatically and scarily broken by the voice of the angel Gabriel: "Your prayer has been heard." This is silence-breaking and history-making. Although we think that the silence means that there is no hope, the words that we continue to silently mouth in our desperation, under our breath, under our sheets, are actually heard by God, even if we do not get the response we think we want, when we want it.

The silence has ended. What will be Zechariah's response to God? You know the story. Because of his unbelief, the silence of four hundred years continued in his mouth. The Advent story is an invitation to break the silence that is the consequence of the sin that stops our mouths, the silence of unbelief that is deafening in its loneliness. The incarnation narrative should be loved for its loudness. When God breaks through and when

Jesus comes, silence makes way for song, and speech overruns the silence. Conversation breaks out everywhere. People do not just speak: the text says they exclaim! The question marks that symbolized all those silent years of disconnectedness and doubt make way in the text for endless exclamation marks of faith. Christ appears and changes the punctuation. The air is filled with loud blessings, and greetings and glorifyings! The first prophetic voice after Malachi is Mary, and the thunder of the Magnificat rolls through the earth. The angelic choir breaks out in full-throated volume.

And it does not end there. The silence was broken by a voice crying in the wilderness, "Behold the lamb of God … repent and be baptized!"; by a voice from heaven that boomed, "This is my beloved Son, listen to Him!"; by a cry from the temple that declared, "I know Him because I am from Him and He sent me!"; by a cry from a Roman gibbet, "It is finished!"; by a cry from an empty tomb, "He is risen!"; by a cry in a garden, "Rabboni!"

The silence of unbelief is undone by the loudness of faith, the silence of separation by the loudness of reconciliation, the silence of solitude by the loudness of choirs singing, the silence of fear by the loudness of friendship, the silence of sin by the loudness of salvation. Please do not feel guilty singing 'Silent Night' - there is a holy silence that signals awe and hushed holiness - but the God of heaven and earth, after four hundred years of silence, is really loud here. The preceding lack of volume was indicative of little affection, little interest, little belief and little commitment. There is a silence that is the result of little love, little faith, and little intimacy. But when Jesus comes, when Jesus is received, when Jesus is worshiped, when Jesus is present, God invites us to join with Him and enjoy the strength of His affections as He expresses them – loudly!

We have got to listen to the text, not just read it. In the same way, we should listen to our hearts. Is there silence where there should be song? One of my favorite prophetic descriptions of God, in Isaiah, is such an appropriate text for the incarnation: "For a long time, I have kept silent. I have been quiet and held myself back. But now like a woman in childbirth, I cry out" (Isaiah 42:14). Supremely, it is in the childbirth of Jesus, that the loudness of God's affections for His creation cries out and breaks our silence.

You get the point. And fortunately, Zechariah ended up getting it too. His silence of unbelief and his disconnectedness from God's narrative, ended when at last he confessed and believed what God had originally said. As soon as he made his confession, the text says, "His mouth was opened and his tongue was loosed and he began to praise God" (Luke 1:64). Where are we at this Advent? How does it find us? Has anything diminished our revelation of Jesus, our walk with Jesus, our intimacy with Jesus? Has joy been silenced? Has witness been silenced? Has worship been silenced? Has prayer been silenced? Has fellowship been silenced? Do we feel like we are caught somewhere between Malachi and Matthew and life feels a bit like that blank page right now? There is no silence of the heart that Jesus cannot fill with song when He comes to us and we are filled afresh with Him. In our Christmas services, we sing songs of invocation like 'O come, O come Immanuel!' When He comes, He gives us back our speech, which means we recover our worship and our prayer and every love-talk expression of spiritual intimacy. If we have lost them, if we have never had them, we can recover them this Advent, even right now, by doing the same thing that dumb Zechariah did, and simply make our confession, agreeing with what God says about us, and what He says about Jesus His Son, confessing our unbelief and receiving His gift of faith, confessing our sin and receiving His gift of repentance and forgiveness. What gifts for such a time! Let us break the silence with our confession, and let the Lord restore to us the loud joy of His salvation!

While the world at large tries to dumb-down Christmas, this is no silent time for men and women of faith. Have you not read the scriptures? "God has ascended with a shout of joy ... the voice of the Lord thunders ... He lifts His voice ... His voice shook the earth ... His voice is like the sound of rushing waters." The Holy Spirit "calls out" and "cries out". From Genesis to Revelation, the response to God's acts of salvation throbs with decibels, all the way to the book of Revelation, the loudest book of all where the sound of heaven is described like the continual roar of a lion, the roar of a great multitude. As Jesus arrived with angelic holy loudness in Bethlehem, breaking the silence, so he will return some day "with a loud shout ... with the trumpet call of God" (1 Thessalonians 4:16). Are you ready for that noise? May this year's celebration of the incarnation increase the volume of your praising soul and tune you just a little bit more, not just in adoring worship of the Jesus who came, but in anticipatory worship of the Christ who is to come. Let the silence be broken by the song of the redeemed. I wish you a loud Christmas!

Last Words of a Dying Shepherd

"And the glory of the Lord shone around them ...
a great company of the heavenly host appeared
praising God ... so they found ... the baby ..."
(Luke 2: 9-16)

Bone-cold I am, dear sir, and weary of this watch
Of blood-shot longing, hunch-backed hope, pale-knuckled care,
Just as I was that pitch and pin-drop night long since,
When he flame-threw His sun into my fireless field,
And eyeless white-light glory, legless flash-flood fear,
Did for a razor-sharp, ice-splinter of still time,
Quite radiate and melt like wax my stonewall heart,
And drown my matted, unshorn, hard-hoof bleating soul.
No question but that peach-soft voice, so grape-firm sure,
Did crook my bolting flight and herd my sheepish fright
Into a pastured peace of good news with great joy.

I barely caught the headlined trust: of David's town,
Of saviored birth, of swaddled sign, of manger-breath,
For in a moment that was a millennium,
There came a distant, wing-fanned, wind-rushed tidal surge
Of rolling, reeling, racing, rising air,
That hotfoot flew like chariots at stallioned speed,
And thudded like the Emperor's armored infantry,
As heaven's host did hurricane its pent-packed praise,
And heavy glory in the highest did cascade
As soft as lace, as moist as morning dew,
To mantle with its grace the favored of the earth.

46

Thus clothed, and with much haste, I found all as was told.
Bear with me, but there are no new, clayed words to shape
A vessel for that sight and pour it out for you.
Tongue-tied, imagination-dried, allow me this:
I would have left the ninety-nine forever more,
To seek, to find, to keep, to love that cradled lamb.
And since that hallowed knee-bent, head-bowed, heart-burst night,
My deaf-blind-lovelorn spirit has but lived to die.
For I have learned that heaven always is that night;
Winged worship, white-wool light, and in the midst, my lamb.
Stone-cold I am, dear sir, and weary of this watch.

> *"I heard what sounded like the roar of a great multitude*
> *in heaven shouting, Hallelujah! ... The glory of God*
> *gives its light and the Lamb is its lamp ... the Lamb at*
> *the center of the throne will be their shepherd ."*
> (Revelation 19:1; 21:23; 7:17)
> (1995)

Sweet and Sweeter

If Zechariah was dumb and dumber, Elizabeth was sweet and sweeter. It is probably unlikely that Zechariah signed to Elizabeth as he walked in the door, "You're going to have a baby." Mind you, it is quite possible that she thought he was a little more amorous than usual. Whatever, the text spells it out: "After this, Elizabeth became pregnant." There is something alluringly and disarmingly gorgeous and serene about this woman. Her womanhood, despite the pain of her infertility, was whole and assured, which could only have been the product of persevering prayer and practical holiness. Somehow, the disgrace she experienced was not able to disfigure her spirit.

Not to have a child was anguish enough, but what was unbearable was the cultural public perception of such a state. If children were a blessing and a reward from the Lord for faithfulness, then it was assumed that barrenness was a judgment, a sign of shame, a consequence of sin. Barrenness was its own kind of scarlet letter. The whirling, accusatory winds and eddying, gossiping currents of imputed shame, combined to weather the soul and erode peace. To bear publicly imposed shame, as well as having to battle the inner skirmishes with self-imposed guilt, is a burden too great. Did she pray the scriptures when she was wordless? "Remember O Lord … look and see my disgrace … Scorn has broken my heart and left me helpless" (Lamentations 5:1; Psalm 69:20). The only relief was that when she could not justify herself she submitted humbly to the judgments and knowledge of God, and trusted Him to be her defender and vindicator. Now, as she touches her blossoming and billowing garments, there is such power in her understated testimony: "The Lord has done this for me." On which word did she choose to put the emphasis? To touch that swelling belly was to feel the favor of God. Grace had a tangible shape and it's presence and power was tactile. Grace specializes in the last, the lost and the least; to those who are on the edge or beyond the pale; to those who believe that "the last train to Clarksville" has indeed left the station and they are stuck in an endless waiting room. He is the God who seems to specialize in the eleventh hour. The part of the rope that He seems to know the best is the end of it.

This was not a cerebral conclusion following a convincing theological paper about the possibility of the miraculous. God's loving-kindness was not some vague essence, some elusive scent in the air. It had a location. Favor had earthed in her womb. How we need to capture the immanence of God's gracious work, the invasion and infusion of His miraculous power. How we need to know that His Word, though a sound that can bring intellectual comprehension, is also a physical force that can bring something out of nothing; that can fling a galaxy and fuel a sperm, and change our lives and circumstances too, why not? No doubt, while Elizabeth was praising the Lord, Zechariah was thinking to himself that he had done quite well too! However you view it, what is happening in these humble circumstances and aging bodies is the very embodiment of that which is to come – the gospel. In a nutshell, God had shown favor and removed disgrace. Was that not how Elizabeth summed it all up? "He has shown His favor and taken away my disgrace among the people" (Luke 1:25). His freeing grace can remove our disgrace in our own eyes, and in others' eyes and in God's eyes.

Does God not still specialize in taking away our shame, when we choose to come to Him as we are, "naked, wretched, poor and blind"? When the last shred of self-respect has been blown off our backs or stripped off us by another, His grace can re-clothe us, and when He does so, His grace is never off-the-rack, but always tailor-fitted to the contours of our need. When the last bit of emotional greenery has been storm-blown from our hearts and we feel like a wilderness on the inside, His grace is still in the irrigation business, watering the deserts of our barren lives. Is that not what Elizabeth had read in Jeremiah: "They will find favor in the desert" (31:2). Had she gone to that prophetic passage she would have found a feast of meditation about all that grace brings: rest (v2), everlasting love and loving-kindness (v3), recovery of joy (v4), harvest and provision (v5), renewed confidence in prayer (v9), stability (v9), deliverance (v11). Did she know the description of favor in Proverbs: "like a rain cloud in spring" (16:15)? Her soul knew that sweet refreshment. Ours can too.

Zechariah's Prayer

"Elizabeth was barren ..."
(Luke 1:7)

Pray, speak to me with angel-words,
And hearken not to my vain litany,
That with legal exactitude recites
Each clause of my contracted life,
Considered, faithlessly, to be
Exclusive to your gavel's freeing grace.

Pray, number not receding hairs and years,
And measure neither tears nor seed
That have been spilled in search of joy.
Listen no more to sterile unbelief
And murmured rage between my childless sheets;
Nor watch dumb lips indict your word.

Pray, chide my frigid, fearful heart,
Constricted, breathless, crushed and self-condemned;
Long weighted by the felled and sapless trunk
Of unconceived, bough-bare desire.
Step not on withered, once green hope
That lies leaf-browned and brittle round my stem.

Stuart McAlpine

Pray, heed not our shamed infertility,
But sprinkle soft your love-moist dew
Upon our sun-scorched, sand-duned souls.
Let tender mercy spring and spray the dust,
Until your fertile will both roots and shoots,
And wells water our wilderness.

"The word of God came to John, son of Zechariah ... in the desert."
(Luke 4:2)
(1990)

Highly Favored

At the very beginning of the New Testament, it is Mary's story more than any other that illuminates our understanding of relationship with the living God. There are two equal and opposite errors in a treatment of Mary, the mother of Jesus. The first is to idolize her and raise her to a status and ministry that she neither sought nor was given. The second, lest the Protestants protest too much, is to ignore her and reduce her significance through neglect and avoidance, through an awkwardness that does not quite know how to handle her, thus failing to appreciate how she is truly representative of all who would know and love and follow Jesus after the Spirit and not after the flesh. What an exemplar of faith and humility we have been entrusted in her story.

From the hills of Judea, the story now picks up in the north of the country. There was no particularly spectacular sunrise in Galilee that morning, nor had there been any strange portents in the sky the night before. When Mary awoke, there was nothing out of the ordinary to give her a heightened expectation that this was going to be a special day. The outside temperature was normal for the time of year and the barometric pressure suggested no unusual atmospherics. It was another day of rounds and routines. She was altogether ordinary to all, apart from Joseph, hopefully. Why? She was his fiancé, so she was almost certain to have at least one nuptial thought during the day. Her family was pleased about the engagement and thought she was marrying "up" as he was "a descendant of David". So it was not as if life was dull because she did have something to look forward to with Joseph, like a baby.

Then there was a sound like the brush of angel-wings. There was a palpable presence. Despite this, it is so interesting to read the almost matter-of-fact way the text gives the details, obviously recorded by a man, not a woman: Galilee, Nazareth, virgin, Mary. For sure, God knows our address and genealogy. His research and knowledge of us is perfect. When He comes to us, He knows what He is getting into, because He knows where we have come from and where we are at presently. What's more, He audaciously asserts that He knows where we can go from here, and what we can be, regardless of the background check that we would have assumed would have eliminated us long since from any possible plans or desires of deity. As we orient to what is happening here, we are always tempted, as Zechariah was, to think that once again the Omniscient One has overlooked something. In retrospect, the virgin status is good, but would it not have been more advisable, because less tortuously complicated, to choose an unengaged virgin, not this "pledged" one. God, you did know she was about to get married?

"Greetings, you who are highly favored! The Lord is with you." I have read that line again and again, as if I was the one who had to say it, and I have to admit it is a real challenge. Try it at home. How does an archangel play it cool and low-key? How did it come across to Mary? If you only go by what was actually said, it should be good news, right? First she is favored, and second, the Lord is with her. What more could anyone possibly want? Clearly, there is something irresistibly attractive to God about a humble spirituality that has no idea how pure and pleasing it is to God, regardless of how it is perceived by others. Again, what a relief it is to be reminded that the Lord knows the heart. So how did Mary respond? We are told how. She was "greatly troubled". Yet again, we see the same pattern. Favor comes but fear comes too. Mary's response to this volley of favor and blessing is probably not much different to that of most people, which is why we can relate so deeply to her. Are we not all troubled when confronted with the extraordinary grace of God when it seems to come from nowhere and does not treat us according to the estimations of our own unworthiness? She was afraid with good reason. Fear is the natural reaction. Why else would Gabriel then say to her, "Do not be afraid."

This might be a good time to ask what our responses are when God comes to us with the good news about the intimate relationship that He wants us to have with Jesus. Or if it can be put it an analogous way – when He asks us to be His mother. Do you remember Jesus' answer to His self-asked question, " Who is my mother?" Pointing to His disciples He said,

"Here's my mother ... for whoever does the will of my Father in heaven is my ... mother" (Matthew 12: 48-50). I think our responses are similar to Mary's, and our fears and potential unbelief can question the conceiving work of the Holy Spirit that would simply reproduce the life of Jesus in us. Like Mary, we can spook for many reasons.

- **His coming is unexpected.** We fear the suddenness of His intervention when He asks us to accept His Word now, without delay. We are unprepared. We are used to silent and non-event living. We have familiarized ourselves with the usual. We have our own versions of the pall of silence that hung over Israel and acclimates us to little expectation.

- **His coming was inconvenient.** God seems to have consulted everything except our calendar. It might not be an upcoming, life-changing wedding like Mary's, but there are plans afoot. Mary was too young. This is an inconvenient time. A simple check on her birth records would have confirmed this, and a check of her medical records would have confirmed that conception was biologically impossible. Maturity-wise, faith-wise, spiritual-experience wise, it is just not good timing. It cannot be convenient if you have not got it all together yet.

- **His coming was unreasonable.** Was there any consideration given to the implications, to the small print, to the cost, to the collateral damage? Had this been thought through by the One whose foreknowledge was meant to be 20-20?

- **His coming was unbelievable.** The fact is, it was too good to be true. (That is precisely the annoying thing about grace and why we opt for the predictable, know-where-you-stand law every time.) What possible relationship could there be between Mary's insignificance and the eternal purposes of God for the entire planet, and for that matter, between the finitude of my irregular life and a divine plan for my existence, now and forever? It is unbelievable.

Yes, it was all of these: unexpected, inconvenient, unreasonable and unbelievable. Yes, she was maritally unavailable, experientially unproven, probably socially unacceptable and possibly unreliable. What I love about our story is that while all these fears are flying and all the possible argumentations are forming, Gabriel just carries on talking without taking a breath. God keeps painting the canvas with those huge brushstrokes of His wonderful affections and intentions. The details of His inclusive love keep pouring out around a fearful heart, apparently unsympathetic to her timorous spirit. She is putting her foot to the floor on her emotional brakes while the juggernaut of God's grace rolls on, delivering the goods like a friendly 'Babies R Us' eighteen-wheeler.

The bottom line here is simple, for Mary and for all of us. Will God's favor and blessing be accepted on His terms or not? It turns out that it is equally wrong to refuse and resist God's acceptance of us, as it is to presume on our acceptability to Him on our terms. Was she really going to keep on pleading any number of supporting evidences to advance her case that she was the wrong candidate for God to choose to love, to choose to use? I am a virgin, for starters, so it follows that I am not a proven parent for the most overwhelmingly challenging mother-assignment of all time, and anyway, I'm engaged so that settles it. The throne of David did you say? I am afraid I have no royalty in my blood, but on second thoughts, I may have a connection soon through my future husband, if we can just put everything on hold perhaps and discuss this after the wedding?

Similarly, the grace of God comes to us all, inviting our acceptance of Jesus, our belief, our co-operation, our submission of spirit and will and intellect and frankly, demanding our all. As it comes it flushes out that litany of exclusive and excluding clauses that scream the unworthiness and unreadiness of our natural state, and every other disqualifying fact of our God-surprised lives. We are in good company because every character in the birth narratives was caught unprepared, and not one of them was chosen because they had it all together. Not one of them was spared the response of faith. It was all about God's initiating grace. Nothing could be more an overture for the teaching of Galatians than this. While the legalistic, pharisaic world hails Santa Claus who is making a list, checking it twice, and finding out who is naughty and who is nice, we choose to celebrate at Advent the outrageous, invasive and explosive grace of God that seeks for us when we are lost and untogether, that finds us just as we are, and that offers us His gifts regardless, all wrapped in Jesus.

How does that grace find us this Advent? How long will we allow our assessment of our life and circumstances to delay our acceptance of God's fertile imagination for our future? How long will we allow the evident limitations of our own capacities to raise a halt sign to the abilities of God's Spirit in us to advance His work through us? How long will we choose to live with unforgiven sin, or live without the grace to deal with the consequences of forgiven sin? How long will it take before it dawns on us that this was never about "some things may be possible for me" but about "nothing is impossible for God"? Who we are, where we are, how we are, becomes the very vehicle for God's favor and grace. A virgin cannot make herself pregnant, anymore than we can kick-start our own spiritual life with the jackboot of our own efforts. We need another to fertilize our soul.

Mary was not chided for asking a question or stating the obvious objection. She asked, "How will this be?" It was a reasonable question, but she stayed to hear God's answer, and Gabriel responds respectfully to it with as full an explanation for divine obstetrics as was possible. Mary catches her breath and her response now is breath taking for us. "How will this be?" melts into, "Let this be". We are now asking, "Let this be, how?"

I have named the poem that follows, 'The Denunciation', partly to show how thin a line it is between a godly annunciation of God's will and a bad denunciation of it. I pray that we will all be able to speak to Father God this Advent as Mary did, and that our spirits will indeed be freshly graced.

The Denunciation

"How shall this be?"
(Luke 1:34)

How can I be, my Lord, what you would ask of me?
Bear with impertinence that would dare to relate
The obvious to One who knows all mystery,
Yet whose omniscience has overlooked my state.

How can it be, my Lord, what you have said of me?
You speak of what will be as if already done.
I would not doubt omnipotence so brazenly,
But facts dictate an unwed virgin bears no son.

How can I be, my Lord, what you require of me,
Unproven, unprepared, unpoised and but a girl?
And what of him to whom I am pledged trothfully?
What shame and blame, what costly accusations will they hurl?

How can it be, my Lord, what you would do in me?
Pray, stay rebuke and timid faithlessness forgive.
According to your word my heart would let this be.
I bid all self-will die, that Christ in me might live.

How can you be, dear one, what He would ask of thee?
But hush the vain disclaimers of your fearful will.
Each imperfection and impossibility
Is known, yet Love insists that you be chosen still.

"Be it unto me according to your word."
(Luke 1:38)
(1999)

Mother Mary – Let It Be

As a teenager in the sixties, I belonged to an overly keen youth Bible study and fellowship movement in England called 'Crusaders'. One looks back and shudders at the name. What I remember is that the way we sang the choruses before the Bible talk had no similarity whatsoever to the lusty howling with which we belted out the latest Beatles hit on the way to that class. I remember one Sunday afternoon the sheer noise of 'All we need is love' and I do not think we were thinking about the love of God at that moment. Our chorus singing was not quite as vibrant and voluble. As a contemporary of the 'fab four' I have always been interested in the way that they have been cultural and generational markers, mostly for ill I fear. So it was with some anticipation that I took a recent voluminous biography of Paul McCartney on vacation for my beach-book. It is always fascinating to learn about the inspiration of certain songs, and that summer I learned about one of McCartney's most loved and timeless compositions: 'Let it Be'. When he sings, "Mother Mary comes to me" he is not having an ecstatic Catholic vision of the mother of Jesus, repeating the words she used post-annunciation. He is recalling a favorite saying of Mary, his much beloved mom, who was always able to be a calming influence "in times of trouble". Was that not when the song says she came? So we have a 'Mary', we have 'trouble' and a 'Let it be', but how different is the meaning of these elements in our story, where our 'Mary' was 'troubled' and ended up saying the same thing.

Our Mary's "Let it be" is qualified. It does not mean: I guess I'm stuck with it, there's nothing I can do about it, I'll just have to put on a brave face, I'll have to be strong and not show any emotion, there's nothing you can do about it, put up with it but don't let it get you down, grit your teeth and grind it out, leave it alone and it will go away, walk away and pretend it's not there, leave it to fate, let them have their way, don't fight it, it is what it is, c'est la vie. All of these are the spawn of the ultimate demonic counterfeit to the will of God that is the idea that the will of deity is deterministic and fatalistic, and utterly impersonal.

Gabriel's words following the greeting included a loving, affirming answer that sought to allay fear, and repeated the blessing of favor upon her, in case that had not sunk in the first time it was spoken. With gentleness but firmness, he declared what was going to be. Listen to the language: "You **will** ... you **are to** ... He **will** be ... The Lord **will** ... His kingdom **will** ..." There are an awful lot of "will's" there. What relates them to each other? They are all one and the same thing – they are all the will of God that will come to pass. Mary is not trying to be precocious when she then says, "How **will** this be?" given that she is a virgin. Gabriel's answer is essentially more of the same: "The Holy Spirit **will** ... the Most High **will** ... the holy one to be born **will** ... Elizabeth is **going to** ..." Anybody who is anybody will! The problem in human terms is that you can 'will' all you want but that does not guarantee that what you want will happen, particularly if you have pre-decided that what you will is just not humanly possible, and is therefore not going to be. The future is going to catch up with those 'wills' and ignore them. Gabriel's last sentence is the crucial comprehensive cover: "Nothing **is** impossible with God." God's will that has to do with what is in the future for us, and presently impossible to us, is an eternal present reality with God that is already as good as done. If I can put it this way: His 'will' (future to us) is an 'is' (present to Him). The human anticipation of what is to happen is presented as the divine action that has already happened. What we have reason to be unsure about is a sure thing with God.

Mary's response is sheer grace and beauty. Now you can understand exactly what God knew about her, and saw in her. Is there any better model of discipleship to follow in scripture? I think not. "I am the Lord's servant." Is this not the essential description in the rest of the Bible of any and every follower of Christ? Notice how she answers. She does not answer in terms of what she 'will' agree to do. She does not join all the other agencies whose wills have been mentioned in the last two minutes of angelic conversation. Having heard what everyone else 'will' do or 'be', is it not time for Mary to respond in the same register? Something like, "I

Stuart McAlpine

will do it ... I will be available ... I will be co-operative ... I will be your surrogate." She does not even say, "I will obey." It is not that she is not being obedient – she certainly is – but the point is that nothing she says is about the agency of her will at all, in a manner that would suggest that it is about what she is bringing to it, about what she is going to be responsible for. "May it be to me according to your word." Though this at first sounds passive, there could not be a more active, submissive reception of a message than this. She is not saying, "I obviously cannot win against all that is willed so let us go along with it with a good attitude." The exercise of her will is simply to open herself up as fully as she is able, in order to receive absolutely whatever God wills to do to her, in her, through her, with her. Her will is fully active and co-operative in this submission. It has not been subjugated, obliterated, or unwillingly controlled. She is saying "I will" as a lover would, affiancing herself to God to bear His Son. Was there ever a sweeter surrender, a holier submission, or a purer trust?

This was neither a mindless, nor a mind-controlled choice. We know that she had questions and asked them. There are three responses of Mary, among many, that are worthy of all of us in the face of any revelation that asks something of us.

- **She was trustingly inquisitive**. Her honest, humble inquiry is a tacit acknowledgement of willingness to co-operate despite some immediate befuddlement about details. She was not sexually ignorant. She knew how things were supposed to work. She knew the normal explanations of this world, the naturalistic ones. But she does open herself up to other information and to other explanations, including supernatural ones.
- **She is submissively obedient.** She offers herself as "the Lord's servant." She is not holding on to either her own definition of herself, or her own self-determination. "Let it be to me." In other words, she can only be what that word makes her to be. That is it. She makes an unconditional choice to trust God's conditioning word regardless of outcomes, likely or imagined. According to her faith? No, that was weak and tender. According to her experience? No, that was pretty well non-existent. According to her support from synagogue, family and friends? No, she was running the risk

of being severed from all of these. According to how good she was feeling right now, what with an angelic experience and all that? No, she had reason not to feel good about the prospect of being considered immoral and the subject of titillating village gossip that was going to suggest who the father might be. According to her physical strength and capacity to endure a pregnancy? No, her body would be tested and her emotions tried, for she had no previous benchmark experience to be her guide. All the props were removed apart from the Word of God, the same word that went forth in the Genesis creative act; the word that has the power to maintain and govern whatever it creates.

- **She was prophetically worshipful.** Had the psalmist not said that God perfected praise in the mouths of babes? Mary's song that we know as the 'Magnificat' is a massive 100 per cent proof confession of the trustworthiness of God's character. Long before her baby cries, let alone speaks a divine word, she proclaims her acceptance of the nature and power of what God wills and works out in His kingdom. She speaks on the basis of God's Word, and on the basis of the definition of the world according to that Word. Her worship is basically singing the Word, totally according to the Word. We have already mentioned in an earlier meditation the Psalmic nature of the Magnificat. Her allusions to the Psalms include: 18:46, 22:3, 25:6, 34:2-3, 71:19, 71:22, 89:10, 89:18, 98:3, 99:3, 103:1, 103:17, 105:8-11, 107:5, 107:8-9, 113:7-8, 138:6, 147:19. This is overwhelmingly indicative of the Word that was hidden in her heart. She declares an assessment of life according to the divine purposes revealed in the Word, and that explains the maturity of her prophetic utterance that is not born of aging years but informed child-like faith. She has not given birth yet. She is not out of the woods. She has not begun to engage the suffering of that promised sword, but yet she sees everything that God has promised as good as done. He has been "mindful", He has "done", He has "performed", He has "lifted up", He has "filled", He has "helped", He has "remembered" (Luke 1: 46-55).

Advent means 'coming' or 'arriving'. Yes, it is about the coming of

Christ to us, but first came the announcement of that coming to Mary. We are now invited to come ourselves to the same revelation, and come the way she did, according to God's Word: trustingly inquisitive, submissively obedient, and prophetically worshipful. I think our song will be more like Mary's in Nazareth, not Mary's in Liverpool. "When I find myself in times of trouble / Mother Mary comes to me / Speaking words of wisdom / Let it be … to me according to your Word." But are we ready for the stretch-marks?

Mary's Men

"Joseph ... took Mary home as his wife."
(Matthew 1:24)

He chose to love me as I was, my dear,
Bowed broken by the stones of public shame.
He placed his life between my faith and fear,
And bore the strikes of scorn and stripes of blame.
Despite my state, his virgin I remained;
He trusted all that deity had done.
I knew that for this child he was ordained,
For do they not say "like father, like son"?

He mantled me with homespun strength, my dear,
And thawed the chills of nine-month anxious care.
He coaxed my pregnant joy and chased each tear;
His silent meekness melted gossip's glare.
So when they saw my mangered darling's face,
Those strangers who beheld Him, one by one,
And saw pure innocence, and tender grace,
No wonder they said "like father, like son".

He always was our pride and joy, my dear,
And yet I felt strange heart-stabs as He grew.
Unsummoned in my dreams there would appear
A sage who said a sword would pierce me through.
He learned the trade: He hammered, chiseled, planed,
And finished tasks no sooner than begun.

His hands were scarred and calloused, sinewed, veined,
But do they not say "like father, like son"?

The people hung upon His words, my dear,
He told them stories never heard before.
He spoke about a kingdom that was near,
Announcing that He was the key, the door.
I used to hide beneath a shaded tree,
Not knowing whether I should stay or run.
At home His brothers could no more agree
That we could still say "like father, like son".

I pondered all within my heart, my dear,
Sins were forgiven, nature was controlled;
The blind would open eyes, the deaf would hear;
Before Him demon power would loose its hold.
And yet they killed my firstborn, hung Him high;
They caught Him in the web their lies had spun.
The reason why they said He had to die?
He dared to claim that "like father, like son".

I must confess I lost my way, my dear.
I thought back to those things I had been told:
Truths learned by wise men, garnered by a seer,
And heard by shepherds watching in a fold.
My weeping was distracted by a cry:
'He's risen - death is conquered - heaven's won!'
Then I remembered, 'Son of the Most High.'
Truly, my dearest, "like Father, like Son".

> **"He will be great and will be called**
> **the Son of the Most High."**
> (Luke 1:32)
> (1989)

Pre-Natal Class

There is something tender and pastoral about the way that Gabriel answers Mary's reasonable question: "How will this be?" Six months before this moment, Elizabeth's pregnancy was the sign that favor was on the move. It was to this miracle that Gabriel immediately referred after letting Mary know that her son's father would be God and therefore He would be the Son of God. It all seemed perfectly logical if you think about it – not! To rein in her incredulity, at the same time as providing some ground for believability, Gabriel says: "Even Elizabeth (yes, even that really old, barren, past-it relative of yours) … is going to have a child" (Luke 1:35). At this point it sounds as if he is compiling a 'most unlikely women to get pregnant' list, except Mary and Elizabeth needed to be on different lists: women who could not get pregnant but did, and women who should not get pregnant but did. Was Mary meant to feel some consolation in this? Was it now easy for her to contextualize? "What a relief you told me that, Gabriel – I feel so much better and totally normal now. Elizabeth? Now that's really weird." It is Elizabeth's miraculous pregnancy that now becomes the most available apologetic for Mary's immaculate one. "She who was said to be barren is in her sixth month." The fact that they are related, provided such a necessary bond of trust at such a needy time.

The conception of John was the sign for Mary that what was happening to her was attested and approved. Elizabeth's miracle was not a terminus for her own enjoyment but a through station for another's blessing. The meeting of these two women represents one of the holiest time capsules in scripture. Who could be trusted with Mary's nurture and discipleship? Who was sufficient to be the mentor of the mother of our Lord? It is quite overwhelming. Did Mary go to Elizabeth so quickly, only because of what Gabriel had mentioned, or did she already know something of the holiness and integrity of this woman that could be trusted? Does it not encourage you to pray that God could trust you with the nurture of others? Is anybody coming your way? If not, why not? How gracious of Father God to closet Mary away from others and prepare her spiritually before her pregnancy started to show and the gossip started to fly.

The short account that we have is enough to let us know that this get-together was saturated with the presence of God. As soon as Mary walks in the door, the Holy Spirit falls on Elizabeth. Gabriel had previously told Zechariah that his son would be filled with the Holy Spirit from birth (Luke 1:14). Did he remember to tell Elizabeth that? She knew it now, as that fetus somersaulted within her while it was being baptized in the Holy Spirit. Here is the woman who was denied, despised, sidelined and rejected, exclaiming "in a loud voice … why am I so favored?" Grace upon grace soaks them both. Long before the Acts of the Apostles, here is a tutorial in the gifts of the Holy Spirit. Elizabeth prophesies blessing on Mary, affirming what God had done in her. Elizabeth's pregnancy was amazing enough but you would hardly know she was pregnant with her own miracle, given her total absorption, focus and excitement on Mary's news. This is not sentimental but spiritual. This is not merely a justifiable, shared, mother-to-mother congratulation. Elizabeth is moving in the Spirit and discerning and responding "after the Spirit" and not merely "after the flesh". Her designation of Mary as "mother of my Lord" says it all. She is the first human to name what God had done. How this holy volubility of faith contrasts with the dumbness of her husband's doubt. Mary is not just an observer here, or a listener only. Luke places the prophetic declaration of the Magnificat in the context of this meeting. Was there ever a combination of being filled with the Word and with the Spirit? Is this an overture, or what?

Herein is demonstrated something about the true nature of the miraculous. It did not draw attention to Mary, but to the Messiah, to Jesus. With every verse you can understand why God had chosen Elizabeth, and why he had prepared her for this trimester, which had as much to do with the nurture of Mary's spirit, as of her body. Her humility is sheer loveliness. There is not a hint of jealousy or assertion of position or prerogative. There is not a smidgeon of threat. She makes no demands for the rights of her child. There is only a joyful submission that expresses itself in pure worship, as mother and fetus do obeisance before an unborn Christ.

There is another thing that speaks to all generations that is easily missed. In a sense, what happens here is that as a mother, Elizabeth prophetically initiates, develops and plays out the role that her son is going to have. She is the model for "forerunning." When her son one day says, "After me will come one more powerful than I" (Mark 1:7) and shares that he must decrease and this One will increase, he expresses a decision that his mother made a long time earlier. And is it not equally interesting, that a mother who said at the very inception of conception, "may it be to me as you have said" (Luke 1:38) would have a Son who one day would say, "Not my will but Thine be done" (Luke 22:42). Because Advent is such a traditional time for family, and often a multi-generational gathering and celebration, would it not be good to consider the influence of the decisions of one generation upon the next, and the influence of a parent's character and obedience on their children?

In the pre-natal class of the Holy Spirit, Mary was clear about this: "The mercy of God extends to those who fear Him, from generation to generation" (Luke 1:50). This recalls the teaching of scripture about two familial facts: there is a **relationship** between generations that cannot be negated; there is a **responsibility** of one generation to another that cannot be neglected. Generations are conditioned by the decisions of earlier ones: by their preferences, by their practices, by their priorities which are usually evidenced by what they sacrifice for. Deuteronomy 29:29 speaks of things revealed by God to a generation that "belong to us and our children." Here is a transmission and transference of goodness, of spiritual giftedness and blessing. Proverbs 4:26 tells us that the one who fears the Lord in his generation will have a secure fortress (spiritual security not social security) and "for his children it will be a refuge." Here again is a tremendous generational spiritual blessing with real life effects.

As we look through Elizabeth's window again this Advent, and listen in to this pre-birth class, let us respond to the call of Isaiah 58:12: to raise up "the foundations of many generations" and that includes the establishment of our own foundation. The best place to begin to do that is the place that Mary started at – the scriptures. The child she is bearing is going to be the extender of mercy to generations. In the midst of the cycles of all our changing and changeable generations, we need to note what has remained the same and what is good and always available for every generation that Mary addressed. Of course, it is the changeless God of creation, the God of all generation and regeneration. Jesus came as the fulfillment of all these scriptures, which you can now make the infallible basis for your advent prayers for your family. Was Mary thinking of these promises from her Jewish scriptures?

- "His faithfulness is to all generations" (Psalm 119:20);
- "My righteousness and salvation will continue from generation to generation" (Isaiah 51:8);
- "Though father and mother forsake me, the Lord will receive me" (Psalm 27:10);
- "Your dominion endures through all generations" (Psalm 145:4);
- "Your throne endures from generation to generation" (Jeremiah 2:31);
- "God's covenant is for all generations to come" (Genesis 9:12);
- "Your memory is perpetuated through all generations" (Psalm 45:16);
- "His name I AM by which I am to be remembered from generation to generation" (Exodus 3:15);
- "Keeping covenant of love to a thousand generations who love him and keep his commands" (Deuteronomy 7:9);
- "The plans and purposes of the Lord stand firm through all generations" (Psalm 33:11);
- "Your renown endures through all generations" (Psalm 102:12).

Truly, the generative life within these Spirit-filled women was going to declare God's mercy from generation to generation. Where do you enroll for this pre-natal class?

The Hourglass

*"She wrapped Him in strips of cloth and
placed Him in a manger."*
(Luke 2:7)

Wrapped in strips of cloth

In a burrowed cave

Red and wrinkled

J
E
S
U
S

Resurrected

From a borrowed grave

Reaped from strips of cloth

(John 20:6)
*"Peter arrived and looked in
at the strips of linen lying there."*
(1983)

71

Mary and Lucy

A few years ago, as the Advent season was under way, two unlikely protagonists dominated the media in December. The New York Times suggested that it was not just a struggle of good and evil but a $200 million smack-down between the religious right and godless Hollywood. The reference was to the competition between current movies featuring Aslan and King Kong. Tongue in cheek, it was noted that though Aslan would appear to have the advantage of omnipotence, that would not guarantee success at the box-office. Of course, the critics could not handle the spirituality of 'The Lion, the Witch and the Wardrobe', so cast aspersions on Lewis and compared him unfavorably with Tolkien, whose 'Lord of the Rings' trilogy had been completed a couple of years earlier. The fact is that Lewis was engaging a completely different world and audience. When Tolkien described the Narnia stories as "woodenly allegorical" he could not have been further from the truth. Allegorical? No. Analogical? Yes, but the thoughts and memories that are stirred in Narnia do not present themselves as doctrinal statements, but as longings for a forgotten country, for a much needed friendship.

The sounds, the scents, the touches are evocative: the smell of Aslan's incensed breath in the air, the hissing of Mr. Beaver's freshly caught fish in the frying pan, the glug of Mrs. Beaver's marmalade roll. Above all, there are the inexplicable feelings that come when it is said that Aslan is on the move. But what has all this got to do with the Advent story, you might ask? Aslan said, "I shall be glad of your company tonight." Isn't the story less about Bethlehem and more about Gethsemane? "The Stone Table was broken into two pieces ... and there was no Aslan." Is it not less about the incarnation and more about the atonement? Does it not fit an Easter meditation better than an Advent one?

I am looking for a wardrobe door into the story of Christ's birth. Allow me to slip through the furs with Lucy into the place that was "always winter and never Christmas." That is a perfect image for the historical and personal terrain we have already been encountering in the gospel narratives. The White Witch's wolves were no less than the Roman legions that ground their heel into the Jewish spirit, and her murderous megalomania was no less than Herod's. The despair of the beavers was earthed in Elizabeth's womb and the hopelessness of the fauns was mouthed in Zechariah's dispirited prayers. The Narnians' longings for Aslan were more than matched by the desperation of Messianic hope that had languished in silence for so long. Isaiah described Narnia well: "gloom ... distress ... people walking in darkness ... living in the land of the shadow of death ... the warrior's boot ... the oppressor's rod" (8:22 – 9:5). Faith was frozen with no thaw in sight. The land of Israel was Narnian. So where does Lucy come in?

You have only been reading the story one minute when Lucy says, "What's that noise?" In another reading-minute, she is alone in a room that had nothing in it except one big wardrobe and a dead bluebottle on the windowsill. It is Lucy who first stumbles into Narnia. She "felt a little frightened, but she felt very inquisitive and excited as well." It is Lucy who bears the shame and reproach of not being believed. "The others who thought she was telling a lie, and a silly lie too, made her very unhappy." Lucy first discerns the nature of Aslan and discerns the relationship between his awesome power and gentle grace: "Terrible paws, thought Lucy, if he didn't know how to velvet them." It is Lucy who first expresses "a horrible feeling as if something were hanging over us ... either something dreadful that is going to happen to him or something dreadful that he is going to do." She watches afar off, weeping as Aslan is mocked and jeered. It is Lucy who scrambles to be the first to reach and touch the leaping back-to-life Aslan. "Oh, you're real, you're real! Oh Aslan!"

Surely you are thinking about all the similarities of Mary's experience, especially as her story also begins with a fearful question of the "What was that?" kind. And did she not also feel a palpable presence? Lewis presents Lucy with this capacity to recognize and receive revelation. It is Lewis who mirrors the birth narratives in the receptivity of women to mystery and glory. When Mrs. Beaver stops what she's doing and stands up and shouts, "So you've come at last," we have to feel that she would have fitted well into the pre-natal class at Elizabeth's house. And when she exclaims, "At last! I never thought I'd live to see this day," we would not be wrong to think of Anna. Particularly though in Lucy do we discern an analogous presentation of the spiritual DNA of another young girl, also in a frigid Narnian landscape – none other than Mary, the mother of Jesus. If Lucy, in this fairy-tale, leads the other characters in the way to approach and respond to the coming of Aslan, then more so does Mary in the original draft of the faith-tale, in the way to approach and respond to coming divinity, to the gift of revelation and salvation, to the wooing of God, to the brooding of the Holy Spirit. "Be it unto me according to your Word."

The story of Mary no more ended at the manger, than Lucy's did after her first trip through the wardrobe. In John's gospel we read, "Near the cross of Jesus stood his mother" (19:25). Mary not only accepted the incarnation, she accepted the cross, which means that in the words of the disciple who took care of her, she acknowledged that this was "the atoning sacrifice" not only for her sins or our sins "but the sins of the whole world." She knew all about the Stone Table. Do we also have a relationship with the Christ of the manger? Do we also have a relationship with the Christ of the cross? It was here that she saw the fulfillment of that incarnation prophecy that He would save His people from their sins, and that salvation was prepared in the sight of all people.

But Mary's story does not even end there. No doubt she was among that group of women that went to the tomb to take spices. Can you imagine the emotions of her heart as she came to terms with Jesus' resurrection and anticipated a relationship with the risen Christ? And then we follow everyone to the Upper Room where we read that the disciples joined in prayer "along with Mary the mother of Jesus" (Acts 1:14). That young trusting teenager had come a long way, and it is sad that she only surfaces for most people at Advent. What is the point? Our assurance about Jesus, like hers, is not only premised on the acceptance of His incarnation, on the acceptance of His saving work on the cross, on the acceptance and experience of His resurrection, but also on the work of the Holy Spirit. Mary was among that number upon whom the Holy Spirit fell. Most often you see depictions of Mary with a halo around her head. How about a tongue of fire upon it? And what about her declaration of the wonderful glories of Jesus in another tongue? Mary, in whom Christ was once carried, would now know that she lived in Him, and He in her, because she had received His Spirit. Wow! It is interesting that Douglas Gresham, Lewis' step-son, shared that Lewis kept Father Christmas in the story, despite Tolkien's objections, precisely because he wanted some analogy to the Holy Spirit that gave gifts of empowerment and healing. Do you remember the sword and shield for Peter, but the gift of the healing vial for Lucy?

It is not enough to only understand Mary and relate to her in the context of the Nativity. Her life and belief, her acceptance by God and assurance are discovered at the same places that all of us must visit and make our own. This Advent, we should visit them again. Let us go to a barn where Jesus came to us; to a hill where Jesus died for us and as us, in our place; to an empty tomb where we too were raised with Him from the power of death and sin; to an upper room where Jesus gives His Holy Spirit.

Yes, I think Mary would have related very much to Lucy and vice versa. She knew what it was to walk with Aslan through the dark woods to the Stone Table, but mercifully, beyond the cracked table and beyond the ransacking of the White Witch's castle. Mary would have more than agreed with the way that Aslan portrays the character of her Son in His gentleness and strength, in His kingship as "lord of the wood", in His life as creator, as well as redeemer and sustainer. The fact is, that when you come through the doors of your church for your Advent services, you have walked through the wardrobe as it were, into a personal encounter with our Aslan, Jesus Christ, who was incarnate by the virgin Mary, was crucified for our sins, raised for our assured redemption, and was the Giver of forgiveness and the gift of the Holy Spirit. May these gifts always be received by all of us at Advent.

(You will understand the connection between this meditation and the poem that follows.)

The Lamb Roars

*"You are a lion's cub, O Judah ... the scepter will not
depart from Judah ... See, the lion of the tribe of
Judah has triumphed ... Then I saw a Lamb ..."*
(Genesis 49: 9,10; Revelation 5:5,6)

Blind, bloodied, bowed, old Israel's gnarled hands blessed
The young whelp, Judah, untested, untamed,
Yet destined to become the bearing loins
Of lionesque and messianic hope.
And as the longing, so did that cub grow.
Isaiah heard its growl, Amos its roar;
The wild beasts dared not rouse Him from His crouch,
And nations could not rein or leash His tread.

I never entered the Professor's home,
Or saw a dead blue-bottle on the sill,
Or smelt stale mothballs falling from dank furs.
I never walked through such a wardrobe door,
Into a white-witched, snow-bound wintered waste,
Or ate my fill of sweet Turkish Delight,
Or battled Orknies, Ettins, Cruels and Hags.
No Spectres, Minotaurs or skirling pipes.

But I have journeyed in a different land:
The scorched savannah of the parched-dry soul,
Where beneath skies blackened by vultures, bats,
Lay carcassed hopes and skeletal beliefs.

Yet there one day I saw the grasses bend
And watched a mane of tousled glory glide,
And felt the tremors from those velvet pads.
And did I say I have heard Aslan's roar?

I silent sweated, fretted – hidden still.
Asudden, through the flora of my fears,
That haunched-spring power leapt and landed firm.
Unblinking liquid eyes soft-pierced my soul.
There was no thought of paws, or jaws or claws;
As wants and wishes wept away their need.
I felt that breath that some said melted stone;
I've ridden, on that back, the Spirit's wind.

And yet this ruling lion of Judah's tribe,
That once inexorably stalked its way
And staked with holy spoor its earthly claim,
Just vanished from the earth, believed extinct.
So who would think that such a kingly beast
Would return clothed as lion in sheep's skin,
To be the most humble of all the pride.
Messiah, Lion of Judah, Lamb of God.

> **"Then in the name of Aslan, said Queen Susan, if ye will all have
> it so, let us go on and take the adventure that shall fall to us."**
> (The Lion, the Witch and the Wardrobe)
> (2012)

Not Your Average Joe

I once heard a guy ask, "Why does Advent seem to be mainly for women and kids?" Is that a fair question? How does a man relate to a manger? Why do Men's Ministries not have Advent evenings the way that Women's Ministries seem to do? Maybe guys could swap beer mugs, and then have a seasonal winter lager. Should guys feel disconnected? Of course, there are plenty of men who get into the story, but there are still too many who do not, which is strange given that the incarnation narrative is a rich resource for understanding male spirituality, and how men get engaged by God in His purposes.

This story is as inclusive as you can get because it was the inclusiveness of God's love that was of such importance to Dr. Luke. That is why it is all about women, and Gentiles, and outcasts and anyone who had appeared to be excluded from God's grace. Folk seem to stumble into the story, every which way, from every which angle. Some come:

- suddenly and unprepared like the shepherds;
- on a hunch like the wise men;
- after years of longing and searching and waiting like Anna and Simeon;
- with simple trust like Mary;
- with a joyful and relieved surrender like Elizabeth;
- from a place of rank incredulousness and unbelief like Zechariah;
- with initial doubt and rejection and with a struggle like Joseph.

But come they do, and come we all may in similar ways, but come we must. How did you come to Jesus? Which of the above do you most relate to? And if you have never come to Jesus, which of the above approaches best defines how you might be coming?

Let us focus on that last guy I mentioned, and his way of coming to Jesus, his way of becoming connected. In Matthew's gospel he is actually the very first of the disconnected, the unenlightened, the unprepared that we get to meet, so he requires our attention. After the opening genealogy in Matthew 1, Joseph is the one being written about. You might think, 'Any name but Joseph!' We are thinking Ordinary Joe, Average Joe, Joe Bloggs, Joe Schmo, Joe Blow, Joe Sixpack – what is it about Joe? Why has Joe become Mr. Run-of-the-mill-middle-of-the-road? Why not Mike or Bill or Jack? Why is it always Joe? 'Why me?' was certainly on Joseph's mind as these events erupted. The meaning of Joseph's name is: 'May Jehovah give increase' or 'May He add'. Your "increase" usually referred to your children. So he has an "increase" to look forward to – or maybe not.

Let's face it. This is hardly a great beginning. After all, this is not a fairy tale. We first find Joseph with his world in ruins. The exploding mortars of misery are falling fast: disgrace, divorce, dread, doubt. "Before they came together, she was found to be with child." Joseph was described immediately as a "righteous man" so we know that they had not been sexually "together". It is the ultimate horror. The girl of his dreams, the one he is engaged to and about to marry is pregnant, and it is not his child. This is bad in any circumstances but particularly in Jewish culture, because engagement had the equivalence of marriage given the seriousness and solemnity of the covenant promised – thus the use of 'divorce' in the text and not 'broken engagement'. Of course Joseph would want to know who the father was, and of course, whoever it was, would be the focus of both disgust and anger. Mary's attempts to console him with the news that it was God would not have helped. She was not only immoral; she was now blasphemous and possibly insane.

As the implications of these facts broke in on him, what was his response? Was it deep sadness for being rejected? Was it anger for being cuckolded and humiliated? Was it suffocating shame for appearing publicly to be the immoral fiancée who could not wait? Was this an inexpressible tragedy for him, or was it a last minute reprieve and deliverance from one so promiscuous, irreligious, deceitful and generally unstable? The total mix of shame, ridicule and disappointment is in his face. Yet as we read the story and watch him try to respond, we already know that everything he was reacting to, that appeared so disastrous, unacceptable and unbelievable, was in fact truly and righteously the work of God. Surely, even if Joseph did for a minute allow the possibility that Mary was telling the truth, the problems are not solved. If the biology of it all was problematical then what about the theology? What on earth is God doing in heaven's name, the God whose eyes are meant to be too pure to behold evil? What is He doing messing with Joseph's virgin? This hardly looks pure. Joseph could be forgiven the thought that God, if He was for one moment possibly responsible, must be a terrorist of legitimate hope and longing. Why me, why this, why now, why her? What are you doing God? Who are you? What do you want of me? Are these questions familiar?

As this Advent story continues to teach us, the ways and workings of God do not always at first present themselves to us as tailor-made to our passions, plans and perceptions of what ought to be. The revelation of Jesus, for this is exactly what this is all about for Joseph, was going to require some things of him, including things that would not conform to the expected norms of what was considered social or cultural, or even reasonable and appropriate.

Think about it. This beginning of the greatest story ever told is outrageous and problematic. That a virgin would bear the Christ is shocking enough in terms of wrapping your mind around an immaculate conception. But Joseph's contemporaries were not going to come to that conclusion, any more than Christ's peers. Can you imagine the humor down at the local hostelry when word got out that it was God? Immaculate indeed! Forever, in that culture, Christ was going to be slurred and smeared with the ignominy and shame of illegitimacy. From the very beginning His origins were in doubt. The rumors of an unsolved and mysterious tryst, of strange dealings, of potential doubt, would continue to linger and challenge faith. So why am I indebted every Advent to Joseph, the first guy on the narrative scene? Let me suggest some reasons.

FIRST I am indebted to Joseph because I have only been reading the New Testament for two minutes, and he teaches me how to respond to the workings of God that I cannot fathom immediately with my rational mind and my usual discernment and savoir-faire. I really understand his initial response. Get out of there. Run. Do not touch it. Yet it is clear from the text, that as with Mary, we begin to see exactly what God saw in him, and why He could trust Joseph with such an initial shock. There was something about him that remained trustworthy even when his trust had been shattered. Note that his motive for wanting to "divorce her quietly" was to protect her from as much public disgrace as possible. He cannot cover her presumed sin – it will show soon enough – but he did try to cover her shame. Do not forget that he has been dragged into the shame. He was shamed by Mary, who he assumed had slept with someone else, but as we have already suggested, everyone would assume that he was the one who had slept with her, so the shame was on him. They all knew how it could so easily happen. His testimony was blown. His righteous life was tarred and feathered. Even thirty years later, we read of Jesus, "He was the son, **so it was thought**, of Joseph" (Luke 3:23). Did you hear a little uncertainty there? Yet despite his own sense of public nakedness, he still tries to do what is as right as possible, given how wrong everything appears to be. Could it get any worse? Are these the circumstances on which the salvation of the world hinges? Really? The worse the mess happens to be, the greater the miracle of redeeming deliverance. But that is only ever a retrospective view, not a present perspective. Precisely because it begins in a mess, I think most of us can relate to the process of recovery and discovery, because we do not begin our spiritual pilgrimages at a place of pristine order or understanding either, though few would experience anything approaching Joseph's confusion.

The text simply says, "after he had considered this, an angel of the Lord appeared to him in a dream" (Matthew 1:20). He is in the middle of a living nightmare and now he has a heavenly vision. It never rains but it pours! "Do not be afraid." It seems to be the opening word for everyone because it really is scary stuff. It is first a word to him and about him, before it is even about Jesus. How incredibly personal is the love and care of God, that He should first console, comfort and confirm Joseph before proclaiming the main piece of pressing news. The message corroborated Mary's story. There is no record of a long conversation, or of Joseph besieging the angelic visitor with questions in his own aggrieved defense. We read, "He did what the angel of the Lord commanded him" (1:24). Which was what exactly? It was to take "Mary home as his wife." But would that not confirm the public assumptions about his sexual guilt? Was he not taking responsibility for this child? In taking Mary, he took Jesus.

Why do I love this man, this poster boy for godliness? I love him because he chose to identify with what God was doing, with who He was doing it with, regardless of how it looked, or how it would effect his own public reputation or sense of personal dignity, or prospects. To accept Jesus, to accept salvation on God's terms, has always been about counting the cost, about running the risk of being considered a fool, a laughing-stock, by the watching world. Before it was ever said of Jesus that he humbled himself and took the way of no reputation, we see that modeled in his "lower-case dad", his surrogate father. Again, we see what God saw in Joseph's heart all along, in the same way that God discerns the potential of any heart that is responsive to Him and that will trust His word.

The text says that he awoke and "took Mary home as his wife." He could not have identified with God's work anymore intimately or anymore immediately than that. Did not Jesus himself use that idea of being taken home by us, as the image for intimate relationship with him? "We will make our home with him" (John 14:23). It was all a walk of faith that defied the odds. In putting his arms around a pregnant Mary, he embraced the will of God beyond his understanding. Then he had to live with it, in all its implications, day in and day out, watching that maternal bump get bigger and bigger, or to put it another way, watching the purposes of God for him in Jesus Christ just grow and grow.

Then there is that most intimate of revelations. "He did not know her until she had brought forth her first born son." He had no sexual intercourse with her until Jesus was born. And do not forget that for three months of her pregnancy she was apart from him with Elizabeth. This speaks volumes of his voluntary, self-denying, God-preferring response to the will of God, in a manner that put the purposes of God's work above his own, including the legitimate ones. Why do I love him? First, because he teaches me to trust God beyond what my eyes see, beyond what my sense is telling me, beyond what my fears suggest, beyond what the public demands.

THE SECOND THING I love about Joseph is that he becomes the first example in the first gospel of what a true disciple is really about. He is described as a "righteous man". In other words he did what was right by

God's standards, regardless of the cost to himself personally, emotionally, sexually. You cannot arrive at God's will for your life by choosing your own route. He models a walk of faith against the odds. He is everything that Jesus later described as a disciple. How much honor of Joseph was there in Jesus' presentation of what made for a man of faith? Little did Joseph realize, in those early steps of bewildered obedience, what it was that God was going to entrust to him. Would he later have said it was all-worthwhile? Will we, despite the hiccups and stutters, the deprivations and sacrifices, the limitations and aggravations, and all the frustrations that are the consequences of holy choices? It was not a cloistered walk for Joseph, for it was undertaken in the glare of village gossip, the scandal of shame, the mockery of others' cynicism. "So how are you doing, Joe? Immaculately, I hope!" In effect, this was pioneering the path that the child he would nurture would one day walk Himself. Like father, like son. You ask me why I love him? He teaches me what it means to walk by faith and not by sight; to be a disciple who seeks first the kingdom of God and His righteousness.

THE THIRD THING I love about Joseph is that he got to name the child. It is such a lovely touch in the script. When Jesus was born it says, *"and he* (that's our Joseph) ... and **he** gave Him the name Jesus" (Matthew 1:25). Are you kidding me! If I were God I would not have allowed such a thing. There would have been a light show in the firmament like no other with a heavenly voice like no other booming the name from the starry stratosphere with a cohort of angels doing a fly-by and the name Jesus appearing in their exhaust. I would want no one to be in any doubt that this was my boy. But the God of heaven defers to Joseph, and invites him to specify who this boy is exactly. If you had spoken to Joseph a few months earlier I think he would have named these circumstances very differently, and in particular, named that fetus a number of choice, unkind and uncomplimentary things. Like Zechariah, it is all about this business of naming. Do you remember what you named your circumstances and life before you were aware of God's loving purposes for you? What are you naming your circumstances now? Is the God who is getting too close for comfort being named as fear, or threat, or trouble? God invites us, as he did Joseph, to name these circumstances and feelings differently, and discern what is really going on. O the stretch-marks of faith, the discomforts of

Christ. Years later there would be a similar set of circumstances for Jesus' disciples when they got caught in a storm out on Galilee. Some only named the circumstances as a life-threatening storm. Peter named it differently. He saw the Lord in it and walked on the water. Why do I love this man Joseph? He teaches me to discern the work of God in my life, and invites me to name what is going on as God's work and initiative pursuing me. There is so much in my life that did not rest well with me when I first perceived it, but later, with Joseph's help and example, I was able to name it 'Jesus': Jesus wooing me, Jesus disciplining me, Jesus refining me, Jesus redeeming me, Jesus convicting me – frankly, Jesus saving me.

At one moment Joseph was despairing of his life and future. What a change God brought. What blessing followed when he surrendered to the Lord and listened and obeyed the word to him. He chose to co-operate with God against sight and sense and there he was, prophesying this name over the child, for the salvation of all generations. Why do I love him? Why is Advent a guy's thing? Because Joseph shows me how God can take a faithless and fearful guy and give him a faithful and bold ministry. What an exchange! Who would have guessed?

As we keep asking, where does this Advent season find your life? Are there pains and struggles in walking out the will of God? Are you tempted to run and quit on this possible relationship with Jesus? Is God trusting you with your responses to His faith-stretching requests and requirements of you? Are things happening in your life that are anything but the dream circumstances you had planned for and to be honest, it looks as if resolution is as far away as the delivery of that baby seemed to Joseph. Are you bearing shame and humiliation in this process? Are you learning, like Joseph, to continue to co-operate with God's pregnant purposes and trust His delivery date? Are you choosing to respond as Joseph did, righteously not reactively, and in obedience, doing nothing less or more than what God has shown you, though it may neither feel nor look good? Is your character being tested and honed as Joseph's was? How would Joseph counsel you? I think he would say, "Dear-heart, there is one simple and indisputable thing that makes it all worthwhile – relationship with Jesus, a revelation of Jesus, the presence of Jesus in your life. Don't run. Don't check out. Don't doubt. Don't delay. Just come. Take Him on. You may be naming it many things right now – name it the Lord! Take Him home." Thanks Joe! You are an Extra-Ordinary Joe, and I do love you.

The poem that follows was provoked by Simeon's description of Jesus as a child destined "to be a sign" (Luke 2:34), and summarizes my personal response of deep gratitude to what Joseph has taught me.

To Joseph

(who taught me how to look at art)

"This child is destined ... to be a sign."
(Luke 2:34)

You did not frequent marbled shrines
Or marvel at the brush-stroked lines
And contours of museumed artistry.
No guided tour, no catalogue,
No philosophic dialogue
In Nazareth – no civic gallery.

Yet you beheld a work of art,
The making of a holy heart.
At first its meaning was so hard to see.
The artist said He was divine,
That earth would bow before His sign.
But is art pure that robs virginity?

Joseph, you taught me how to view,
To look by faith and sight eschew,
And give the artist time to be believed.
When flesh-framed masterpiece was done,
It flamed the image of a Son.
When hung, at last its meaning was perceived.

(1986)

Postscript For Joes

Joseph has remained a mentor of my life. I am always overcome by his capacity to give God the most precious gift of all, time. I mentioned my gratitude in the poem you just read. He allowed God to be the God of time, to do what He willed, how He wished, when He wanted. To surrender time to God, to embrace consequent patience, long-suffering and even plain suffering, is to enter the heart of worship, the quiet center of whatever hurricane may be blowing.

You may be a Joe who needs to follow his example and trust what God has done in Jesus, in His birth, His death, and His resurrection for you; trust what God is doing in your circumstances; co-operate with Him and not resist the way He is drawing you into the gravitational pull of Jesus' friendship with you. The last line of the poem says it all. Indeed, when hung on that cross, the purpose of God's masterpiece, Jesus, is perceived. Do not turn off the road like Joseph was tempted to do, and settle for a quiet alternative. Do not divorce the love of God. It is worth dealing with the shame of what we would rather not face, than live a life of unresolved blame before God. God is calling us all again, this Advent, to trust Him beyond present experience and present expectations. Like Joseph, in embracing the Christ-child this Advent, let us go all the way, and choose to embrace all the purposes of God in Christ, that include a cross where our sin is forgiven, and a resurrection where our lives are raised to serve Him with joy unspeakable.

A greater than Joseph is here – the one who Joseph named Jesus. Bring your disconnects and dissonances of spirit, not to a manger, but to the feet of a risen Jesus that happen to be nail-pierced. This is where all the fate and fury of circumstance has been excised, where all shame and blame has been borne. Receive a fresh invitation this Advent to follow Jesus to the end of the story, and as you bend your knees, name your life and circumstances as Jesus would. One of the last references to Joseph in the gospels is in Luke 2:33 where it simply says that Joseph "marveled at the things that were spoken of Jesus." Go ahead and join Joseph this Advent, with all the other 'Marvel Men' in the birth narrative, who began the story completely overcome by life, and ended, overwhelmed by Jesus.

The next poem is darker and edgier and catches the extremity and the confusion of the birth announcement for Joseph, but it seeks to present the resolution.

Consensual or Covenantal

"She was found to be with child ... He had in mind to divorce her ... Take Mary home as your wife because what is conceived in her is from the Holy Spirit."
(Matthew 1: 18-20)

Hard-boned coercion or soft-skinned assent?
The covenanted curtain had been rent.
Chaste virtue's uncut cloth – unwrapped and ripped;
Laced love, once veiled and pledged, now plundered, stripped.
The tender seal of innocence was torn
And hidden perfidy would soon be born.
Capsuled in deep-spaced, black-holed dark of grief,
Abducted longings kidnapped sleep's relief.
Fire-furnaced anguish, regret's glaciered chill,
Freeze-dried desire scorched-earthed the fevered will.
The bars of silence requiemed the shame
High-massed the blame, until dawn's angel came
And powder-brushed this grave with grace divine,
Speaking with breath that smelled of barley wine;
Hymning a truth that righted what seemed wrong,
And scripting vows fit for a wedding song:

'I care not how or what you may appear;
I have espoused you as my virgin, dear.
Spiritus Sanctus has such life conceived,
And Christ in you, the gift I have received."

**"I promised you to one husband, to Christ, so that
I might present you as a pure virgin to him."**
(2 Corinthians 11:2)

(1991)

Naming God's Way

The narrative is choc-full of self-descriptions and perceptions, of emotions and conclusions that betray unfavorable perspectives. This pattern is repeated again and again, in story after story, character after character. The beginning of the story has echoes of the beginning of the Old Testament where "darkness was over" everything. The good news is that like the Genesis account, the sentence did not end there but continued, "and the Spirit of God was hovering" (Genesis 1:2). As you walk into the story there are some sharp stones underfoot, words that stub the spirit and bruise the soul. Listen to them again: barren, fear, dumb, troubled, enemies, darkness, no room, terrified, sword, pierce, disgrace, divorce, kill, weeping. Everywhere you look, these words suggest either long-standing present problems or fast-approaching future ones. The personal lives of those in the story are unsettled. Is anyone just waiting to be chosen by God, tank-full of faith, and ready to go? No one is presenting his or her resumé to be the obvious one to be chosen by God. Rather, everyone has a disclaimer. Opposing any possible divine work of inclusive grace, are their own physical, emotional and spiritual exclusive clauses: too old ... too late ... too inexperienced ... too shameful ... too young ... too ordinary ... too bad ... too difficult ... too dangerous ... too much ... too impossible ... too unbelievable. There is not one of us who does not know about the exclusive and excluding clauses of our own definitions of our natural state: our past, our sins, our fears, our failures, our doubts, our indisciplines, our compromises, our bondages, our immaturities, our depressions, our disappointments. Who me? In the story we meet people who have named themselves and others, their present circumstances and their future hopes. These have all been tagged with a label that says: "It is what it is." You live with it. Try and have a nice day, anyway.

All this was bad enough, but even when some wonderful things began to happen and began to be said, the bad naming continued. Zechariah was told how to name the child 'John'. He named it 'inconceivable'. Mary named herself 'virgin' and God named her 'pregnant'. The Holy Spirit comes upon Mary and Joseph named the child 'illegitimate'. God named Him 'Son'. When Mary's village realized she was pregnant, they probably named her 'harlot'. Through Elizabeth, God named her 'blessed'. It is the work of the Holy Spirit to help them all to learn to name things God's way, and Zechariah is a particular case in point. None of us can stand in judgment over him, and all of us should be thankful we have been spared his deserved judgment. We can relate, because we too have had experiences when our faith circuits blew and the doubt flooded in, and with it unbelief. Yes, we have suggested that his dumbness was a serious punishment for a serious sin, but as we have seen again and again in this narrative, where sin abounded, grace abounded more. Where fear ruled the roost, favor freed the coop.

Yes, Zechariah's punishment was just and a chilling reminder that unbelief silences communication, and thus breaks relationship. But was it cold and callous? No, it was not, because the evident grace of God is operative. The dumbness was a grace because it caused him to internalize in the silence and consider. He was saved from more stupidity and agnosticism, and forced into private communion. It is almost as if God silences him to shut him into a school of recovered faith; to lovingly force him to have to think about what he was communicating in writing to Elizabeth, and to confess the unabridged, unedited details of what God had said. I think God knew the pain of his unanswered asking for a son all those years. This is not about shutting him up so much as shutting him in to his answer – to learn to wait for it, to learn to want it on God's terms, not just his. Like all chastening, this was discipline for this senior priest. I think in those silent months he had learned what others in the story also had to learn – to name things God's way. He could not name his identity in terms of his aging flesh. It was not how God named it. By the way, is not the naming work of God the very first thing we hear Him doing on the very opening page of the old creation story? Did He not name the day and the night, the sky and the land and the seas? And did He not name them "good"? The story of the new creation seems to begin in the same way.

So John is born, and everyone is joyfully loud – everyone, that is, except Zechariah. The inability to speak was the shared experience of a really old man and a one-day old boy. At least father and son had that in common. As he silently looked at that baby, how many times did he think back and say, "That was really dumb!" He could only think, "That's my boy!" not exclaim it. The description of the birth and then the *brit mihal* (circumcision) eight days later is so down-to-earth and almost humorous. Everyone is having a good time again (except the baby of course). Here is the mess of ordinary life, and it is business as usual and of course the kid is going to be named Zechariah II. That is how we name it; it is how we have always named it and always will name it. But wait! Deity is about to interfere with cultural and social determinism.

Following the actual circumcision by the *mohel*, the child was sometimes handed back to the mother and the *mohel* or whoever was honored to do the naming would say: "Our G_d and G_d of our fathers, preserve this child for his father and mother, and his name in Israel shall be called …" "No!" shouts a Spirit-filled, still discerning, still prophetic Elizabeth. "He is to be called John!" Is she crazy? Surely the parents spoke about this! (Has anyone heard Zechariah speak lately?) Basically, the objection is: "We have never done it this way before." It is slightly amusing that at this point in the proceedings there are some more furious signings going on. Did that remind Zechariah of something? Zechariah was dumb, not deaf. He asks for a writing tablet and scribes: "His name is John." At last he got to call things the way God did. They knew he was emphatic and this was final just by the way he thrust the tablet toward them. Naming was a prophetic act for Jews. In that name, he prophesied all that Gabriel had spoken. His unbelief had been bled out of his system. He had learned that family genes are trumped by God's grace; that family traditions are trumped by God's truth; that it is more important to be spiritually consecrated than culturally approved. In the recovery of his agreement with God's answer to his prayer, 'loud' happened! His tongue was miraculously loosed and his first words were praise of God. The Word of God was expressed by revelation through Elizabeth but grace found a way to ensure that Zechariah was included. All these characters were learning that grace counts you in when you have discounted yourself out. He was also included in the same experiential encounter with the Holy

Spirit that his wife had savored with Mary. It was not too late. Nor is it too late for us, to have the bondage of our spiritual silence broken by the agreement with God's speech.

Do you know what is really priceless? When he was filled afresh with the Holy Spirit (the reviving of his life that he knew he needed and that he had been longing for) the text says that he "prophesied". Once he named it God's way, the divine intentions for the world that his unbelief had denied, unwittingly became his global mission. We know that prophecy as 'The Benedictus' that is an integral part of the liturgy of the church, both Catholic and Protestant. Since that day of naming things God's way, his words have been a prayer and song, translated into every language where the Christ-child is adored, and incorporated into the worship of the majority of Christian services that have been conducted for two thousand years. O what God can do with the speech of dumb guys who allow God to do the naming! This Advent, accept afresh how God has named you, and how He is naming your circumstances. Remember what John said, that all who received the incarnate Jesus who came to us, and believed "in His name" He gave "the right to become the children of God" (John 1:12). Thus we are born again, and bear His name, and consequently are named son and daughter. If you name Him rightly, you will be named rightly. And to make sure we are named rightly for eternity, "His name will be on their foreheads" (Revelation 22:4).

She Said … I Said …He Said … I Said

"He had in mind to divorce her."
(Matthew 1:19)

"It's Holy God," my Mary said.
The trip-wire of her impudence
With virulence infected sanctity
With violence detonated blasphemy
As treachery heart-bombed integrity,
And terror-blasted my now shrapneled love,
Embedded instantly as shattered memories
Of a long-cherished, since my boyhood, fondled hope.

"It's unclean bastardy," I said,
This fission of reactive pain.
With vitriol and viridescent grief,
With red-eyed rage, I cursed my raped romance.
I called it traitor, felon, fraud and thief.
I slanged the scarlet shame, lambasted lust;
Clenched-jawed, I mouth-fisted the not-to-be-opened
Hope chest of my eternal and virginal dreams.

"It's Holy God," the angel said.
The nightmare of my darkening soul
Was violated by a radiant voice
That firm as rock and vast as firmament
Did with its warding wings sweep clean the fear
That bone-deep vice-gripped my life-throttled breath.

95

Angelic whispers fertilized my neutered faith.
By that same Holy God, was hope conceived in me.

And thus I named it differently.
No longer was it called disgrace,
Despair, divorce, or illegitimate;
No longer cuckold, fornicator, sham,
But righteous, husband, father to a son.
I saw but hopelessness within that womb
Of circumstance, that bore the hope of all the earth.
"It's Holy God," I said. "And Jesus is the name!"

> *"And he gave Him the name Jesus."*
> (Matthew 1:25)
> (2010)

Watch Out for Jimmy

The story is told of children at a church whose Christian Education Director was putting on a nativity play for the congregation to come and coo over. As she later told it, the problem really began at the casting of the main parts. Little Jimmy had a high view of his talent and had decided that only Joseph's role befitted his theatrical ability since, after all, it was the male lead. Sadly for Jimmy, it was Johnny who got that part, and what made it worse for him was that he did not get to star across from pretty Suzie, the sweetheart of his fertile imagination who was playing Mary. Jimmy was assigned the Innkeeper, hardly a stellar role in a story full of every kind of star imaginable. He was a smart kid so why was it that he could not be trusted with a part that demanded the learning of lots of lines. He knew the story in the gospels and the fact is that the innkeeper says nothing directly, simply because he is not even mentioned. Sure, his inn is referred to, but there are no credits rolling for the master of the house. The text just says "there was no room in the inn."

Needless to say, he threw a little fit and was threatened with ejection from the cast. The Director pointed out that such emoting was inconsistent with the kind of feelings they were trying to convey, namely, joy to the world, ding-dong merrily, *gloria in excelsis* and all that kind of stuff. Opening night was a full-house and the Director could not have been more relieved to find Jimmy in excellent form, laughing with Johnny and Suzie and actually wishing them well for their upcoming moment together under the lights. Surely this was answered prayer, a work of sovereign grace, and a sign that the evening's production was covered by divine benevolence.

The Nativity play began, and everything was going smoothly. Praise the Lord! One could already anticipate the final curtain call before all the ecstatic parents, grandparents and congregants. As you well know from your knowledge of the story, the moment arrived when compliance with the decree of Caesar Augustus was required. A booming megaphone voice back-stage pretended to be Caesar making his declaration from Rome, and on to the stage came Johnny as Joseph, leading a very pillow-puffed Suzie as pregnant Mary. Johnny came to the inn door and knocked. There was a long silence.

There was a hush in the audience as every eye was on that door. Johnny kept his wits about him, and like any good actor, improvised and knocked again, even more loudly, coughing under his breath and scraping his sandal on the stage. The door promptly opened with a sudden whoosh and draft of air, and there, resplendent in his peasant garb, stood an extremely beneficent-looking Jimmy. I say Jimmy, because they never even gave him an authentic name – he was just the characterless "innkeeper" on the program, so talking of "no room", there was certainly no room for Jimmy to develop any sense of persona or stage presence as a nameless small-town hotelier. Anyway, I digress. There is Jimmy, for this single moment in the play, the center of attention. Mary and Joseph are secondary characters, utterly dependent on Jimmy. In fact, come to think of it, the entire future of redemptive history is standing on tiptoe, breathless and as expectant as Suzie. After all, they are doing the asking, so the patron has the floor and the upper hand. Jimmy appeared as happy and pleasant as he had been before the play began.

In retrospect, he must have been practicing for this moment, exercising his facial muscles against his better (embittered) judgment. This means that he too was actually a very good actor indeed. As Joseph and Mary stood before his threshold, looking as forlorn as possible, Suzie was panting slightly, but maybe not quite enough to give the impression that Mary was about to go into labor. Jimmy pulled himself up to his full height, inhaled with thespian ardor, and in a loud and authoritative voice, laced with tones of what seemed like kindness at the time, and with eyes that sparkled with what seemed like compassion (though these descriptions of kindness and compassion would later be revised), and with fully inflated lungs and remarkable projection power, he shouted: "Sure guys, there's loads of room, come on in!"

Momentarily stunned, and not knowing what to do, Johnny made a terrible mistake. He stumbled across that threshold pulling panting Suzie in with him, and needless to say, the wheels came off the production. You will be relieved to know that the director somehow got them back out of the inn, and Jesus did manage to get born under the props that had been built to represent the stable. Jimmy was not seen when the actors took their final bow, but of course, it was Jimmy's absence that people saw most clearly. Even though invisible, he dominated everyone's thoughts, and in fact, dominated the production. Johnny and Suzie were never spoken of again, but Jimmy is a man of legend.

Suffice it to say that Jimmy is not alone in seeking to divert and subvert the text, to challenge and undermine the narrative as given. Just a change in one line, one detail – just one deviation, one diversion and you have a different story with a totally different meaning. The scriptural accounts of the incarnation are presented with as concerted and concentrated a presentation of worship, of prayer, of the power and centrality of the Word of God, of the nature of Christ and His redeeming work, of the supernatural ministrations of the Holy Spirit, as anywhere else in scripture. They represent a mother lode of truth. But as much as this persuades us that these texts should provoke in us a renewed and refreshed expectation in our relationship with Jesus, so equally others are persuaded to negate the efficacy of these truths, and thus, in questioning them, challenge the entire presentation of the New Testament. There are plenty of Jimmy's, with all manner of motivations and determinations, standing at all kinds of open doors, inviting us to leave God's script for an alternative route to comfort and ease, to satisfaction and salvation. The inns of heterodoxy and heresy, the inns of theological liberalism and materialistic philosophy, the inns of scientism and existentialism, the inns of selfism and secularism, and all the recently crafted cocktail lounges offering any number of hospitable and socially acceptable post-modern libations, are all seeking to change the road signs, alter the plot, so that Christ cannot possibly be who scripture or Christ Himself, say that He is.

I have used a light story to make a heavy point, simply because somewhere between the Christmas carols and the Christmas cookies, between the punch and the presents, the same things have to be said that have been proclaimed by the voices of the church down through the ages. In the face of all distortions and deceptions about who Jesus is, in the face of all of Jimmy's open doors, we declare in the words of the Apostles'

Creed: "He was conceived by the Holy Ghost, born of the virgin Mary." Or in the words of the Nicene Creed, He is "the only begotten son of God", or with the Athanasian Creed, "the Lord Jesus Christ, Son of God ... equally both God and man." In the words of the Creed of Chalcedon we confess, "that our Lord Jesus Christ is one and the same son, the same perfect in Godhood and the same perfect in manhood, truly God and truly man ... like us in all things except sin; begotten from the Father before the ages as regards His Godhead, and in the last days, the same, for us men and women and for our salvation, begotten of the Virgin Mary ... the same son, only begotten, divine Word, the Lord Jesus Christ as the prophets of old and Jesus Christ himself have taught us about Him and the creed of our fathers has handed down." Instead of wishing each other a 'nice' Christmas, it may be better to wish a 'Nicene' Christmas. Our Nativity scenes may have a cradled Christ but if He is not a creedal Christ then there is no meaning in what is presented.

The meeting of Jimmy with Jesus is continually re-enacted. Most of the Jimmy's, caught somewhere between skepticism and atheism, oppose the incarnation because they have bought in to any one or more of three assumptions, highlighted by Michael Green in his book "The Truth Incarnate":

1. There is no divinity in the writings of scripture.
2. There is no possibility of miracles because we live in a closed box of cause and effect.
3. There is no specialty or finality in Jesus.

That is why godly theologians have labored to articulate a Christology that deals with two equal and opposite questions. First, how can one man give particular form to the absolute God? Second, how can God be tied in any meaningful way to one man?

Defining doctrine has never been a pastime for people looking for a leisure activity, but it has been the passion of apostles and apologists who have vigorously defended the truth of who Jesus really is in the face of all opposing descriptions and corruptions. Given that our times are as dismissive and distorting as any other, we should be those who commit themselves more ardently to truth about Jesus. If you read the

New Testament, it is precisely because the earliest heresies were those that attacked both Jesus' nature and work, that the church saw fit to defend two truths, and this defense dominates the New Testament record. Epistles exist precisely because these truths were being explained and defended. First, Jesus was both God and man. Second, He was one person not two.

Concerns about error here explain the basic requirements of the catechism that John specifies: a confirmation that Jesus came in the flesh and an accompanying confession that Jesus is the Christ (1 John 4:2, 5:1). The gospels present Jesus in His basic humanity and in His essential deity. He lived as His contemporaries did, without any diminution of His Godhead. He was not a ghost, nor was He a good guy who God nominated as Messiah after the fact. He is presented as God in person, but subject to limitations of humanity. This is the way that God chooses to achieve His purposes of revelation, redemption and reconciliation. The fact that the story begins with a baby is sufficient to illustrate the risk, the vulnerability, and the powerlessness that was willingly accepted in order to display what God was really like. Dangerous? Daring? Shocking? Staggering? Yes, all of these. In Christ, God did not choose to outstrip human strength, but strip down to human weakness, subject to suffering but without sin. We are not allowed to forget this humble birth, for it is the notion of becoming a child that is the key to understanding how we enter the kingdom of God in utter child-like dependence.

This is why the rehearsal of the Christmas story, hopefully without Jimmy's participation, is so important. We are not allowed to forget this fragile birth – the fact that if there is any subversion to be enacted, it is that of God who took us from below, by becoming man and undoing the foundations of an unredeemed life. The unabashed scandal of the particularity of Christ's personhood must be declared in the face of all the Jimmy's, whether tut-tutting biological scientists, whether demythologizing theologians, whether new-age cultists. If there is no incarnation there is no salvation. Is it any wonder that the enemy of souls has a vested interest in subverting and humanizing this season? Even if it is ceded that Christ was born, we are required to tiptoe around as silently as possible and treat Him as if He is never going to grow up and learn to speak and have something to say.

The Christ in swaddling clothes is easily coddled. But the mature

Christ of the gospels will not so easily be rocked to sleep. The baby became the man, and the man spoke with words that shock with their claims and power. Jesus' claims to deity can no more be tucked away in the manger, than you can put your pet Blue Whale into your washing machine for a little swimming exercise. The magnitude of Christ's understanding cannot be kept under the stable straw. No amount of Manger-Management will be able to suppress what Jesus said once He got out the crib, past the baby cries and the early speech development phase. Without apology, embarrassment or hesitancy, yet with humility, dignity and assurance:

- He presented Himself as the authoritative Teacher (not saying 'Thus says the Lord' like the Prophets but rather 'I say unto you').
- He used the personal pronoun with consistent conviction ("I am the light of the world ... I am the way, the truth and the life").
- He commanded people to both hear and obey what He said ("he who hears my words and obeys them").
- He called men and women to follow Him ("Come unto me ... Take up your crosses and follow me").
- He testified to an intimacy with God His Father that was His inevitable portion as God's Son ("I and the Father are one").
- He claimed divinity ("Before Abraham was I am").
- He identified Himself so closely with God that response to Him was equitable to response to God ("Anyone who has seen me has seen the Father ... He who hates me hates the Father").
- He accepted as applicable to Himself both the descriptions of the Messiah in scripture as well as the Messianic designations He received from others ("You are the Christ ... My Lord and my God").
- He received confession, forgave sins, bestowed life and healed as a sign of His moral and spiritual authority ("Your sins are forgiven you ... Rise up and walk ... Today you will be with me in paradise").
- He declared that He would judge people by their attitudes and allegiances to Him because eternal life depended on a response to His words ("Whoever believes in the Son is not condemned but whoever does not believe stands condemned").

We really do want Jimmy to have his place in the story, but free from the perplexities of the head and the pains of the heart that would subvert truth and rob him of his place at the final curtain call. To that end, we pray this Advent, that though the inn's door is closed, that we know that heaven's door is as wide open as it was on that night that love came down and glory shone around.

Mangered Margarites

('margarites': Greek word used in the New Testament for pearl)

Father ...

It's said the world's our oyster and that we
Need only speak for our success to be;
That we can shuck ideas and dreams and things
Desired, like just so many pearly strings.

In vain this mollusced life I've sought to prise
Apart. In bloodied hands it clam-shut lies,
And I, shell-shocked remain, and dumb,
Believing not my treasure-find will come.

It's said that somewhere there's a milk-white stone,
That you, in this dark oyster bed did hone
From common grit: sand-grained, salt-soaked, sea-bound.
And did I hear, perchance, it may be found?

Pray, drift me on the current of your grace,
And ease my magi-soul to that pure place,
Where ocean floor is torched by paradise.
There may I find that pearl of greatest price ...

Jesus

"The kingdom of heaven is like a merchant looking for fine pearls."
(Matthew 13:45)
(1992)

Inn or Out

The incarnation narratives, as we have already seen, are utterly realistic and truthful about responses to Jesus, recognizing that not all of them show acceptance and joy. We have noted that Zechariah's disagreement with Gabriel was not a good start, and Gabriel's response was not all sweetness and light. We have seen Joseph teetering on the brink of divorce. Later on, the picture of Mary holding her child to her breast is preserved from sentimentality by the modifying prophecy that a sword would pierce her heart. The rejoicing of Mary's Magnificat that is carried on the wind is counterpointed with the sound of Rachel weeping for children. There are spontaneous adorers but Herod reminds us that there are also assassins. The text says that Herod was disturbed by the threat posed to pride, position and prestige. To some Christ was a troubler, not a treasure. The possibility of His Lordship challenged the thrones of men's making. The impulse to exalt Christ is matched by the one that would eliminate Him.

Responses of both welcome and rejection are recorded. When Isaiah prophetically saw that Jesus would be despised and rejected of men, no one could have foreseen that the rejection would come so early in life. In fact, it began pre-natally, which makes the cameo of the innkeeper so poignant. At the beginning of the New Testament, Christ's experience is of a shut door, and at the very end of the Bible, the glorified Christ is again in front of a closed door, knocking for entry (Luke 2:6; Revelation 3:20). The appeals of Joseph for room for an infant Christ become Christ's own appeals for Himself. What is it about all those hotel signs?

Who knows why we choose the signs that we hang on the doors of our minds and hearts. There are two main ones that come to mind. The first is the neon NO VACANCY sign of our soul. Sometimes it is because we really have chosen to fill our lives with everything in general and nothing in particular, thus assuming a satisfaction, a fullness, a completion that does not even recognize its own bankruptcy when Christ comes knocking at the door. Sometimes it is not because our lives are full at all, but we simply refuse Him room, despite the emptiness, because we do not want His presence, and the possible re-arrangement of personal space that it would require. So there really is room, but it is just easier to turn on the 'No Vacancy' that renders preparation unnecessary. When all is said and done, we have chosen our comforts, tolerate our discomforts, and frankly prefer our own company.

The second sign is familiar to all who have ever stayed at any hotel or hostelry. It simply reads DO NOT DISTURB. Sometimes it even sports an appearance of manners and begins PLEASE. It does not deny that legitimate calls or enquiries may be made. It just denies access for its own private and self-consumed reasons. Some of them may be legitimate in our eyes: our right to spiritual privacy, our right to only relate on our terms to those of our choosing; our right to control relationships and mold the world to fit our lives our way. But then the 'Do not disturb' command can be used to guard an illegitimate privacy, to bar Christ's entrance from what goes on behind the closed doors, dealings that are destructive to self and others. The private hotel room of the soul has curtains pulled and excludes the light from the emotional and visual pornography, from the self-consumption before the mirrors of our own image-making, the emotional affair with self, or the sexual affair with another, or the one night stand with darkness.

Or we can be less exclusive by meeting on the doorstep, though still denying entrance. We are too civil to slam the door in His face, and are happy to entertain a short socially religious exchange, but let us not confuse this with intimacy. Christ at the door can be treated as an unwelcome solicitation. Maybe it is Christ as the UPS guy, Mr. Brown, or as Mr. Mailman – good for delivering certain things I need from time to time but nothing to engage by way of personal relationship. Christ is confined to a religious tradesman but never cultivated as a friend.

Perhaps our responses are not like any of these and far more charitable and relational in our eyes. We give Christ access and He does get beyond the threshold, but He definitely is on our turf, and His movements are limited, and the conversation is controlled. There are plenty of off-limits areas of the heart, including upstairs and the basement. Sadly our Advent services will include many who claim a relationship with Christ but only as a social guest, tolerable when they are available. Others who have let Him past the door would not acknowledge Him as the co-owner, and treat Him more as an impersonal landlord, good for the maintenance of the welfare of the property but not involved in the personal details of house-keeping.

Christ's desire is not to be landlord but Lord, not a tenant but an owner-occupier. Of course there are many fears that lead some to bar and lock the doors to Christ. He never forces entrance. He recognizes the handle is on the inside. Fortunately there is another hotel sign that we could choose to put on the doorknob of the heart. We could flip the 'Do not Disturb' sign and display PLEASE CLEAN THE ROOM. One of the greatest of spiritual reliefs is to realize that we cannot clean ourselves up for His entrance, and in fact, do not have to. He is still in the same towel-and-basin business that He was in when He washed His disciples feet prior to His crucifixion. He comes in to clean, not just the dishevelment of the stuff, and the idolatries of our private chambers, but our own selves. The scarred hands that clean us, remind us that His death on the cross has removed all these transgressions from us and that once and for all we can be forgiven for the mess and be cleansed.

Whatever happened to that nativity innkeeper? Was he ever present when Jesus later taught the crowds? Did he ever hear Jesus tell the parable of the Good Samaritan, and did he shudder when Jesus referred to the innkeeper who did have compassion on the presented need? The poem that follows is an imagined lament from the innkeeper, in which the real one from Bethlehem and the imaginary one from Jericho, are one and the same person. I hope you feel some personal response that opens the doors of your heart to Jesus.

The Innkeeper's Lament

"There was no room for them in the inn."
(Luke 2:7)

Today a man checked in his friend
Who needed time to heal and mend
From wounds incurred in an attack.
The stranger paid, said he'd be back.
As he left for Jerusalem,
My thoughts returned to Bethlehem.

Had I known then what I know now,
I would have found a way, somehow,
To improvise, to make a change,
Re-organize and re-arrange.
How could I know that peace of mind
Would rest on how rooms were assigned?

Caesar's decree was heaven-sent.
While guests raised glasses, I raised rent.
I'd dreamed of such a business boom,
And it felt good to say 'No room!'
How could I know my greatest chance
Of gain would not book in advance?

In any case, they looked unwed.
"Still looking for a flop-house bed?"
I played the crowd, I got a laugh.
"Go find some hay for cow and calf!"
How could I know a barn would be
More fitting than my hostelry?

At last a sullen silence fell.
Nobody rang the desk-clerk's bell.
Yet it still jarred within my brain:
His pleading and her labor pain.
How could I know that God would call,
Wrapped in a pregnant woman's shawl?

I tossed and turned as guilt chased sleep;
I numbered stars and counted sheep.
I dreamed of winged-lights in the sky,
I thought I heard a baby's cry.
How could I know kings don't need sheets;
That sheds make perfect royal suites?

That's more than thirty years ago,
Before we came to Jericho.
No longer do I bar my door
To late-night needs or vagrant poor.
That stranger had scarred hands and brow ...
Had I known then what I know now.

"He ... took him to an inn and took care of him."
(Luke 10:34)
(1988)

Wise Guys

They slipped into the 'Diplomats Only' parking zone in the forecourt of Herod's residence, their bold innocence fortified with a seasoned 'savoir-faire'. They were wheezing with delight at the prospect of a great find. "Well, lads, where is he?" The guards could see from their out-of-state bridles and their up-market safari gear that they were not locals, but their evident class was at odds with their apparent lack of respect for royal privacy. The stage-light brightness of their joy and mischievous excitement served to dispel the darkness of their hard pilgrimage with all its grit and grind. Their unabashed merriment in this palace of man's pretensions, their unselfconscious ease in these corridors of egotistical power, sufficiently represented the freedom and laughter of all the fools of the world who became wise, simply because they took the facts of the birth of Christ at face value.

So who are these wise guys? Various traditions have emerged over the centuries, attaching not only names to the wise men, but details and meanings that are not in the biblical text. Matthew refers neither to "kings" nor to only "three" personages" – that arose because of the mention of three gifts. However, given the nature of the caravan trains that traveled the one thousand miles from Persia at that time, with all the accompanying servants, the group may have numbered about three hundred persons, not three. That explains why they made such an impact on their arrival in Jerusalem. It was public imagination that would continue to provide distinctive personalities to these characters and one thousand years after they lived, so-called relics of the three kings would be deposited in the golden shrine in Cologne Cathedral, via Constantinople's St. Sophia's church and Milan. In the text they are simply described as magi from which our word "magic" comes. A Magus was a priest in Persia, and they were to that nation what the Levites were to Israel. They became the wise men who instructed and trained the kings of Persia. It is interesting to note that many historians argue that because of Daniel, who was appointed as the head of the Magi by King Darius over 500 years earlier, there had been a strange relationship between Persia and Israel and it is not unlikely they were aware of Jewish expectations of a Messiah through Daniel's prophecies. Given the dominant newspaper headlines of our day that present Persia, known by us as Iran, with all its present apocalyptic aspirations, it is amazing to note that from this geography there came a supernaturally directed delegation to find and honor the Messiah of Israel. How incredible is it that the area of Iran would have been among the first to know the good news about Jesus. There is a precedent to pray for that nation.

Anyway, the point is that you will not find Caspar, Balthasar and Melchior in a biblical concordance. However, in most biblical dictionaries you will find discussion about the symbolic meanings of the gifts that have become part of ancient tradition: the gold that represented majesty and kingship; the frankincense that was used in worship representing deity and divinity; the myrrh that was used in burial representing the suffering of the cross that would be necessary for salvation. So these gifts were seen as emblematic of who Jesus already was, but also as prophetic anticipations of what was to come. But perhaps there is another nuance in the text, since in the rabbinic tradition, the Songs of Solomon are all about the joys of God's intimacy with His people and the bridegroom is presented as perfumed with "myrrh and frankincense". These substances were therefore already understood in the Jewish mind as uniquely representative of God's desire for relationship and closeness, an intimacy now intimated supremely in this child, Immanuel, God with us. The bottom line is that in the history of the church, the gifts that these wise men brought became the prophetic summary of the life and death, the ministry and message of Jesus. But they combine to become a sort of invitation card to us, even as we read the story today. Jesus is available, He wants to end separation and distance in relationship with God, and He comes seeking intimacy. But are we wise enough to know that?

So imagine a Presidential-length cavalcade of limousines with Russian number plates pulling up outside the White House and portly fur-swathed dignitaries alighting, bearing an air of impatience, pushing their way through the guard post and shouting, "Where is he?" Would there be any doubt about who they were looking for? Of course, the guards assumed that since this was Herod's palace, it was their Lord and Master that they were after. They were indeed looking for an owner-occupier, but one whose acreage and sphere of influence were somewhat greater. No doubt the Chief-of-Staff was informed and it was deemed politically shrewd to respond to an unscheduled appointment, with possible implications for foreign affairs in the Eastern bloc. How global these implications would be, they never could have guessed. "Herod, is it? Good to meet you. Where is he, the kid that's going to take your throne?" They were wise men, right, so I am sure they did not put it quite like that. When there is a newborn ruler to find, there is no time to waste, bowing and kowtowing to minor tetrarchs. The cosmetics of Herod's practiced political etiquette were definitely smeared. The resident theologians, as godless ones often do, tried to restore the smile of good intentions to the smudged face of evil. Their spiritual obtuseness did not seem to recognize the connections that every child in Sabbath School would have known – Micah's prophecy about a ruler coming out of Bethlehem. How sad it is to have a religious familiarity without any expectation of its life changing power: to know the facts but not their personal meaning. "Where is he, indeed!" echoed Herod. The search to adore Christ and the search to assassinate Him had met on the Bethlehem Road, as they would continue to meet on the thoroughfare of all ages.

The journey of the Magi was not a planned vacation. This excursion would re-arrange their private world forever. They had committed themselves to a venture that their reasonable peers warned them would get them disbarred from respectable intellectual circles. Why sacrifice an established academic reputation, the esteem of friends, the love of family, the respect of the community at large, and possibly your life? As has been the case ever since, the pursuit of Jesus Christ has been viewed by many as anti-sense, anti-social and anti-self. With hopes pinned on a star, their hike must have strained every fiber of their self-judgment and self-respect. Yet so great was their unembarrassed desire to discover the truth for themselves, that they chose to disregard the discomfort of it all. While the smart guys had their heads buried in the old books of the law, doing some emergency research and proof-texting, the wise guys pulled out onto the highway, their eyes longingly raised to a constellation of grace that seemed to move ahead of them.

It is a grand irony that it happened to be the chief priests and teachers of the law who directed the first Gentiles on the scene to Jesus, the same authorities that would later condemn Jesus and crucify Him. These wise men are the evidence that the good news about Jesus is that He was the Christ of the Gentiles too, of those who were regarded as foreigners to the covenant of promise and excluded from spiritual citizenship. God's promise to Abraham about blessing all nations is what the wise men are all about. It turns out that they represent not the wisdom of men, but the wisdom of God that included everyone in His purposes, whether Jew or Gentile. The wise men were leading everyone to the source of wisdom itself, to Jesus Christ.

Years later, Paul describes Jesus as the one "in whom are hidden all the treasures of wisdom" (Colossians 2:3). In his first letter to the Corinthians, Jesus was "the wisdom of God" (1:24), the one who "has become wisdom for us from God" (1:30). Paul has a reason for emphasizing this because the Corinthians prized the intellect. Not surprisingly, it was an intellectual center, and because it was a bridge between the east and the west, teachers of wisdom would travel the trade routes that met at Corinth. It is most likely that Paul was regarded as one of these traveling wise men and this explains why the first four chapters of his letter mention "wisdom" over twenty times, as he tries to explain that the gospel is not in fact what they would consider wisdom in an accepted sense; that they are going to have to revise their understanding of what constitutes wisdom. Paul gets right to the point. The unaided intellect cannot know God, cannot understand the cross and cannot accept the gospel. The Jews, who love signs, and the Greeks, who love speculation, just did not get it.

The story of the incarnation could only be regarded by all of them as foolishness. No wise man would ever be found in the vicinity of this event. To the Jew, convinced in the power-presentation of the Messiah, there was no way that such meekness and lowliness could be the context for His coming. For the Greek who believed that the most prominent characteristic of God was *apatheia* (the word from which we get our word "apathy") it was impossible for God to feel anything at all. The argument was that if God could feel something then He must have been moved to do so by someone, which means that someone greater than Himself had influenced him. Thus a God who would come in any form to suffer was absolutely untenable and a contradiction in terms. It was Plutarch, the Greek historian and essayist, who argued that it was an affront to divinity to think that God could be engaged in human affairs. Such an idea was the epitome of folly.

So you can understand that the very idea of incarnation was totally repulsive to the Greek mind. Celsus was a writer in the second century who viciously attacked Christians and represents this Greek mindset: "God is good and beautiful and happy and is in that which is most beautiful and best. If then he descends to men, it involves change for him, and change from good to bad, and beautiful to ugly, from happiness to unhappiness, from what is best to what is worst." For a thinking Greek the incarnation was absolutely impossible. The wisdom of the world, whether Jew or Greek, could not comprehend the incarnation as anything but folly. Nothing could have less to do with wisdom than this idea. If this is then what folly is, you can understand Paul's words to the Corinthians when he says: "If anyone thinks he is wise in this age, let him become a fool. The wisdom of this world is folly with God" (3:18-19). The wise men who came to Jesus were prepared to become those kinds of fools.

"It stopped." In that motionless moment, an entirely new movement was released. The star had opened their eyes and evoked indescribable longing, but a child opened their hearts and elicited unutterable worship. The world-proof doors that guarded the strongholds of their souls swung wide on their hinges, as they offered their precious treasures. The smell of the myrrh would linger in Mary's memory for many years after it had been lost on the night air, for it intimated sorrow and death, and prophecies unfulfilled. Who knows how long they spent in this communion, but the time came to leave and contemplate the journey home.

As important as the travel routes of philosophical, historical, and even theological investigation are, it is equally critical that like these really wise men, our approach is more than abstract. Martin Luther once described his approach as experiential and devotional, and this is an apt characterization of the way that the gospels present Jesus. They invite us to travel the road with such as the wise men, to look and listen and come to a conclusion.

The conceptual approach is not greater than the one by camel. Luther writes: "The scriptures begin very gently, and lead us to Christ as to a man, and then to one who is Lord over all creatures, and after that to one who is God. So do I enter delightfully, and learn to know God. But the philosophers and doctors have insisted on beginning from above; and so they have become fools. We must begin from below and after that come upwards." Luther's warnings about becoming fools brings us back to the wisdom of the Magi, and our equal need to be wise people who pursue Christ regardless of personal cost and comfort, pride and prejudice, and respond to Christ's own injunction to find out and test if these things that are said about Him are true or not.

Though the Magi's encounter with Jesus is narrated in only three verses (Luke 2:9-11), they capture the difference that meeting Jesus makes.

- "They saw a star ... they were overjoyed."
- "They saw the child ... they worshiped."

To begin with, there was nothing greater to command such attention than the star, but when it came to where Jesus was, by stopping, the star bows out because it is no longer the main attraction. Make no mistake about it, the star was supernatural, but despite its brilliance it was just a lighting effect. One star made way for another, a greater star prophesied centuries earlier: "a star will come out of Jacob" (Numbers 24:17). This star was this child Jesus no less. As it turned out the star was not the light, but it did lead the Magi to what the apostle John would later describe as "the true light that gives light to everyone" that "was coming into the world" (John 1:9). If we just see the star, our affections may indeed be moved, invigorated, and may experience a degree of joy, but that which is the supernatural means to lead us to Jesus, is not the thing itself. It is a tragedy to stop short, by stopping with the star and not moving on and in to the revelation of the Christ.

Sadly, people do stop and worship stars, and allow their lives to be dictated by their assumed horoscopic power, contrary to scripture that commanded us "not to be enticed into bowing down to them and worshiping" (Deuteronomy 4:19). When Israel disobeyed this and "bowed to the starry hosts" it was their end as a nation (2 Kings 17:16). Isaiah warned that "your astrologers ... those stargazers" could not save the people "from what is coming upon you" (Isaiah 47:13). The idolization and demonization of Nature becomes the opposing power to God. The devil may even concede the notion of God as Creator but not as the God and Father of our Lord Jesus Christ, who is lying beneath that stopped star. The natal star perfectly embodies the function and purpose of all creation, pointing away from itself to the living God, captured by the Psalmist: "praise Him all you shining hosts" (148:3). As David testified: "When I consider the stars ... how majestic is your name" (Psalm 8:3). The wise men saw the star, but thank God they saw the child and worshiped. We can be grateful for every means that God uses to bring us to the same place. Sadly, spiritual lighting effects keep many people satisfied on their pilgrimage and tragically they never see the child.

Herod had invited the Magi to drop in for a cocktail on the way home, for old time's sake, and for a further exchange of information to advance diplomatic relations with the new king, you understand. The Herod's of this world have never been known to happily espouse the interests of that other kingdom, and so it was, like millions who would later retrace their steps, the Magi found it impossible to either betray Christ to Herod's world, or to return the same route, having once discovered Jesus. The pained intensity of their outward-bound trip was readily forgotten as they meandered home another way and savored the scenery of another country. For once in their lives, there was no need to find a new travel brochure, for the route they were savoring would roll on to the foothills of heaven, the next oasis for those who, like them, have bowed the knee to Jesus and given Him the treasures of their heart.

The Journey of a Wise (Every) Man

"Wise men came from the east ..."
(Matthew 2:1)

I fell for fork-tongued hissing wiles,
Believing that the tree would make me wise.
I sold my soul for what beguiles,
That damned me darkly deep to folly's guise.

Thus east of Eden, banished, I
Would scan for pin-prick light the pit-bull black,
And curse the eyeless, deaf, mute sky
That mocked remorseful heart-pleas to go back.

Until that "just another" night,
When not just any natal star white-burned
And bade me follow its pure light.
To westward, homeward my steps turned.

I knew where this star-path would wend.
Was that not the Euphrates that we crossed?
Where could this mystery journey end,
But in the glades of paradise once lost?

Yet where it halted, where it stayed,
I tell you neither seer nor sage could know.
A child within a manger laid?
Is this where wisdom would have bid me go?

In Bethlehem, not Eden's joy,
But heaven's pristine glory came to earth;
The second Adam as a boy,
My paradise regained by this new birth.

They called me wise who saw me come,
But I was altogether foolish, dim.
Before I worshiped, I was dumb.
I had no wisdom when I first found Him.

I wide-eyed waited through the years.
I followed His signs now, and not a star.
Until the day when I once more wept tears,
And watched a Roman gibbet from afar.

My mind raced back through centuries,
To Eden's shame and Satan's lies.
I fell again upon my knees.
At last there was a tree to make me wise.

"The message of the cross ... Christ ... the wisdom of God."
(1 Corinthians 1:18, 24)
(2009)

Of Wise Men and Virgins

Jeremy Paxton, for many years a dominant voice in British news broadcasting, was an intelligent and witty cynic and a dry observer of the human condition. As an agnostic, commenting on Christmas, he suggested that it should be cancelled because of the evident shortage of wise men and virgins. However, he did concede that there were plenty of asses that might just keep the show on the road. Yes, this is a little irreverent, but he was more right than he realized, but for different reasons than those he was thinking about.

At least there were wise men at the first Advent. We have seen that they were the trailblazers who invited us to discern the true nature of wisdom. What were their wise decisions that now seem to be in shorter supply?

- *"Where is the one?"* (Matthew 2:2). They unashamedly inquired about Jesus, determined to find out the truth about Him for themselves, despite possible mockery. That was wisdom.
- *"The star they had seen in the east went ahead of them and stopped over the place where the child was ... they were overjoyed"* (2:9). They pursued undeterred till they found Him. That was wisdom.
- *"They entered the house"* (2:11). They took the necessary steps to cross the threshold and on bended knee, come into the geography of God's kingdom and the gravitational pull of Christ. The search was ended by their submission. That was wisdom.
- *"They opened their treasures and presented Him with gifts ... they worshiped Him"* (2:11). The revelation of Christ sprung the latch

of their hearts and they opened up their treasures, but it was themselves that they opened up to Jesus. That was wisdom.

- *"They returned by another route"* (2:12). Once they found Christ it was impossible to leave the same way they had come. It was the beginning of a new journey that required a new route, so they left their old road for a new path. That was wisdom.

Indeed, Paxton was right. What we need today are more wise men and virgins. It could be argued that what follows the birth narratives in the gospels is all about the true nature of wisdom; about what it is to be a wise man or a wise woman. It also happens to be about what it takes to be virginal: to live a consecrated life, to know what it is to recover sanctity and cleansing after a loss of innocence. And the link between these two remains the same as in the incarnation story – Jesus. It is not without significance that Luke ends his account of the birth narrative with the words: "And the child … was filled with wisdom … and grew in wisdom" (2:40, 52). One of the things that the crowds would later ask was: "Where does this man get this wisdom from?" (Matthew 13:54)

A gift that you could give yourself this Advent season would be to take time in the coming year to go through the scriptures and discover what they say about the constituent elements of spiritual wisdom. What are the evidences of wisdom? What are the fruits and consequences of wisdom? If you desire wisdom you will do that. Equally I wish there was time to take you to all the scriptures that teach us about Christ's redeeming power to deliver us from our spiritual faithlessness, from our spiritual adulteries, from our broken, estranged and divorced relationships with God, and cleanse us from our sins and render us virginal again. In fact, Paul when writing to the most sexually permissive culture of Corinth, describes the people in the local church there whose lives have been radically changed by the power of Jesus Christ, as those who had been "espoused as a virgin to Christ" (2 Corinthians 11:2). Once you lose your virginity, it can never be recovered. For Paul, it took that image to describe the transcendent power of Jesus to make old things brand new. Become one of those wise searching men or women as you search the scriptures, for the reason that Paul gave Timothy: "the scriptures are able to make you wise unto salvation" (2 Timothy 3:15). Become a wise virgin.

Remembering that this Holy Child became the Teacher, it might be worth reminding ourselves this Advent of something that He said about a wise man, and about a virgin. He told a story of two men. One was a fool who built his house on the sand and the other was wise and built upon the rock. You know what happened. When the storms came, one fell and one stood. Jesus is unequivocal when he distinguishes folly from wisdom. Who is the fool? The one who hears Jesus' words but never receives and applies them in practice. That will describe the many who will leave another year of Advent services, content to consider only a Christ who cries like a baby, but not the Christ who spoke the words of life. Who are the wise? They are the ones who are obedient to the words of Christ and responsive to the claims of Christ upon them. It is the difference between a life and a death; between keeping and losing; between living on a secure foundation and being subject to the winds of change that blow souls like tumbleweed.

The process for us is strangely similar to what we observe of the wise men in Matthew's account. The text says they entered the house. Like them, at some point, we have to choose to come to Christ on bended knee, simply because we want to submit our lives to Him. Like them we open the treasures of our hearts in worship, unashamedly giving all that we are to Christ. Our wondering and our wandering come to rest on the terra firma of His acceptance and forgiveness, His grace and His love. Built on the Rock, we are ready for the storms that beat upon the house.

Talking of readiness, that is the theme of a second parable that Jesus told, that had to do with virgins – ten of them. Again, He describes the difference between wisdom and folly. They were all waiting for the bridegroom to come out of his chamber so they could accompany him with their lamps to the celebration. But five of the ten virgins had not brought any oil with them and at the crucial time, having fallen asleep on the job, they missed their moment. It is a story about another advent that demands our consideration, and that will as surely come as the first, for which the first was a preparation and invitation to be ready for the second. If the first parable asked us if we were wise, and had founded and anchored our lives in the truth of Jesus, thus ready for all that happens in this life, then the second parable asks us if we are virgins whose lives, whose lamps, are filled with the oil of God's Holy Spirit, trimmed and ready for the life to come.

I am saying that the Advent story about wise men and a virgin has a resonance that comes right to us, right now. It is still about wise men and virgins. Are you a wise person in accepting the reasons for the first advent? Are you a wise virgin, accepting Christ's appeal to be ready for His second advent? This Advent, do not be wise in your own eyes but be a wise builder of your life on the rock, Christ Jesus. Do not be self-righteous in your own eyes, but be a virgin who lives for eternal relationship with the Bridegroom that is Jesus.

Jeremy Paxton did not allow for any of this, and therefore had no idea just how many wise men and virgins there really were. Thus the message of Advent continues, persuasively and powerfully, along with the ... donkeys!

Virginity and Wisdom

"The virgin will be with child ...
wise men came from the east ..."
(Matthew 1: 23; 2:1)

Your coming
then
as a baby
Lord
you were a long time coming
and did not a young virgin bear
and were not wise men gathered there?

Your coming
now
as a bridegroom
Lord
you are a long time coming
and will there yet be virgins then
and will there be five wise in ten?

"At that time the kingdom of heaven will be like
ten virgins who took their lamps and went out to meet the
bridegroom ... five were foolish and five were wise"
(Matthew 25: 1-2)
(2007)

Anna Dearest

When Mary's song burst into air, she praised the mercy of the Lord that extended from "generation to generation" (Luke 1:50). The birth narratives present a multi-generational cast. How I have come to love the grey head of Anna. I call her 'darling', I call her 'dearest', and I call her one of my 'mothers in Israel'. Thinking about her at Advent solicits tears. She has moved my heart, and she has won my heart for more of God. Yet an apposite biography title for her might be 'Incognito'. In some ways she is the lost one, not of course through any lack on her part, but because she is just not on anyone's radar screen, except God's. Heaven's revelation of who figured 'large' in God's version of history will be so different to how we have recorded who did what. Anna is lost to the system, and ironically comes from the tribe of Asher. You got it – the lost tribe. There is not a single ruler or judge in the entire recorded history of the Old Testament who came from the tribe of Asher. Anyone would have assumed they were lost to the purposes of God.

As with the other characters in the story, the stark realities of her life are presented. She seemed to carry the tribal DNA, lost in time and to time. Her biological clock had long since struck. She would appear lost to the grief of a long widowhood; lost to marriage and men; lost to productive community; lost to hope after all these years of longing for God to do something – lost to all but God. For decades she had been hidden in the Temple, and she remains invisible until that extraordinary, strategic moment when she turns a corner and comes into view of everyone who has ever read the Scriptures for the last two thousand years. This moment, this pivot, this hinge of God's history, was the moment she had been preparing for all her lovely life. The text says, "Coming up to them at that very moment" (Luke 2:38).

In the Pentateuch, there are prophetic blessings spoken over Asher. Jacob says: "Asher's food will be rich; he will provide delicacies fit for a king" (Genesis 49:20). Then before his death, Moses' final blessing on Asher was so strong and affirming: "Most blessed of sons is Asher; let him be favored by his brothers ... your strength will equal your days ... The eternal God is your refuge and underneath are the everlasting arms" (Deuteronomy 33:24). Suffice it to say that Anna is the extraordinary fulfillment of a word spoken centuries before, perhaps without her even sensing any connectedness with God's plan during those silent years. That word said Asher would serve the king, and be most favored. Did she ever serve a king – the King of Kings as it happened! And surely her strength equaled her years. There had been no prophet for four hundred years and the first one actually mentioned as such in the new dispensation was a woman – this old woman.

Despite appearances, despite there being no evidence that anything was happening, despite the apparent confinements of her own life, despite her isolation and limitation, despite the apparent lack of influence and fruitfulness, the text simply says that she "worshiped night and day, fasting and praying" (Luke 2:37). She oozes seasoned sanctity. Disconnected and isolated? She was deeply and intimately engaged with the God of the Universe, the God and Father of our Lord Jesus Christ, no less, and as the Father, He had invited her in to the inner sanctum of His revelation about His Son.

This is why she suffered yet bore no traces of bitterness. This is why she aged alone yet wore no wrinkled despair. I wonder how many times she prayed the scriptures, especially the Psalms, and trusted God not to forsake her when she was old, so that she could declare His power "to the next generation", and His "mighty acts to all who were to come" (Psalm 71:18). Surely she must have taken courage from Psalm 92:14 that describes her perfectly: "The righteous planted in the house of the Lord will flourish in the courts of our God. They will still bear fruit in old age; they will stay fresh and green." At the beginning of the New Testament, we are given a picture of a full-time, 24/7 intercessor. The child she had prayed for would take up that role for eternity. Her story and her song, in the words of Fanny Jane Crosby's hymn, was "watching and waiting, looking above; filled with His goodness, lost in His love." That had always been her blessed assurance.

At over one hundred years of age, her life was still all about seeking God, speaking to God and speaking to others about Jesus. A silent, solitary, old lady? She was firing on all possible spiritual communication cylinders.

And what about you this Advent? Maybe you will be one of the older ones at the family celebration who has seen it all before. Generationally, you can at least relate to Anna. How about spiritually? Perhaps most of what you see is now in your rear-view mirror. I love that the last thing that is said about Anna is the answer to her prayers: "She spoke about the child to all who were looking **forward** to the redemption of Jerusalem" (Luke 2:38). Her perspective was prospective. Yours can be too. It is not too late to join Anna's prayer group and like her, speak to a new generation of things to come, not least of which will be a New Jerusalem "coming down out of heaven from God". You can explain that the reason that voice from the throne could say, "Now the dwelling of God is with men" is because a long time ago, the redemption of Israel that was spoken about by a very old lady, turned out to be that child she got to see with her failing sight, no other than God who "became flesh and made His dwelling among us" (John 1:14). Do you not love how God kept her alive to see His Son? Could we be as expectant that passing years will bring an increasing revelation of Jesus to us? Dear one, like Anna, you are on His radar and your calling is still sure. You can afford to wait years for the prophetic timeliness of God's tasks for you. There is so much purpose and specificity in your present placement, as narrow as its confines may appear to you to be. Like Anna, may you too be wind-blown by the Holy Spirit, and have many experiences of "coming up to" those who God has prepared for you to bless. And do not forget, she is simply described as "giving thanks to God". Gratitude will keep you joyful. Despite many years lived, may we be able to ask with the poet George Herbert, "Thou hast given so much to me – give one thing more, a grateful heart." Now that sounds like an appropriately seasonal gift to ask for. It will keep us in Anna's company this Advent.

Tell Me, Anna

"There was a prophetess, Anna, the daughter of Phanuel, of the tribe of Asher. She was very old; she had lived with her husband seven years after her marriage, and then was a widow until she was eighty-four. She never left the temple but worshiped night and day, fasting and praying. Coming up to them at that very moment, she gave thanks to God and spoke about the child to all who were looking forward to the redemption of Jerusalem."
(Luke 2:36-38)

Pray tell me, Anna, what grandparents saw
And sought that they would name your father Phanuel,
Which signifies 'the face of God' no less.
What was it that their hearts yearned to express?
Did they anticipate a fleshed Immanuel
While gazing at their child with reverent awe?

Pray tell me, Anna, born of Asher's line,
Whose given name speaks of delight and fortune's good,
Once prophesied by Israel to bring
Rich delicacies fit to serve a king.
Asher, most favored by his brotherhood,
Promised increasing strength when years decline.

Pray tell me, Anna, why they named you 'grace'?
What brooding intimations mantled mother's heart?
What hopes and fears began to prick and prod
Her prayers when consecrating you to God?
Did intercession spare the guileless suffering's dart?
Would purity indeed reveal God's face?

Pray tell me, Anna, did you ever think,
Widowed so soon that you would affiance God's will,
Then lifelong chaste chase His desire
With ceaseless worship flaming love-ache's fire?
And all alone, did you believe that you would feed your fill,
With prayer and fasting as your meat and drink?

Pray tell me, Anna, after all those years
Of prayer-walked miles on cold, unyielding temple stone,
What was it on that day that firmed your tread?
What sudden gust of Holy Spirit torqued and led
You '*at that very moment*' to be angel-blown
Into young parents' hopes and old man's tears?

Pray tell me, Anna, what within you burst
As your rent soul artesian-sprung a life of joy,
Penned-down and plea-packed for so long it seemed?
You proclaimed Zion would be now redeemed,
And prophesied to all that it would be this boy
Whose consecration would undamn the cursed.

Pray tell me, Anna, let me hear you say,
That you do know unmarried wombs are not in vain,
That midnight travail was not without birth.
For now, my precious, over all the earth,
The children of your supplicating labor-pain,
As taught by you, give thanks for Him this day.

Pray tell me, Anna, darling, let me hear
That my presumption you will tenderly forgive,
That dares to name you intimately so.
Could Asher or Phanuel ever know
Their seed would serve a king and see God's face and live?
Could you have known this son would call you 'dear'?

(2004)

The Irrational Season

Christmas is the time of year that Madeleine L'Engle once described as "the irrational season". So much that goes on just makes no sense. To point out the utter secularization of Christmas is to state the obvious. Some time ago I happened to be in Birmingham, England, where for the sake of religious pluralism, the mention of Christmas had been civically banned in favor of the celebration of "Winterville". That same week, a newspaper front-page story reported that an Anglican Vicar had been forced to apologize publicly to outraged parents of the upper social classes, whose children had been emotionally pillaged by his suggestion in a children's service that there was no scientific evidence for the existence of Santa Claus. I will not bore you with the physics of it all but suffice it to say that given what Santa has to do in the time allowed, the sheer speed of the operation would leave him, together with elves and reindeer, in minute shreds scattered across the galaxy. It struck me as amazing that the very same people would pay their clergy to continue to spread their good news that God does not exist. A cleric can pronounce that and never be asked for a public apology. On the contrary, he will be hailed for his post-modern enlightenment.

I am not seeking to ruin anyone's Christmas or be publicly pilloried for being a social spoilsport, but the fact is that Christmas has never been the major Christian festival. Two of the four gospels do not deal with the birth narratives. Do not misunderstand me, the nature of Christ's birth is absolutely fundamental to our belief and gospel, but the fact that He came must be accompanied by the proclamation and explanation of why He came. That is why, at our Christmas Candlelight services of Carols and Readings, we need to hear scriptures that present Jesus as Savior. He was not a revelation of godliness, but of God, who did not leave it to others to give the reason why He came. It was Jesus Himself who told us why He came, thus making it a rational season:

- not to bring peace but division
- to be the living bread so those who partook of that bread would live forever
- to testify to the truth
- not to abolish the law and the prophets but to fulfill them
- not to call the righteous but sinners
- to bring fire on the earth
- not to do His will but the will of the Father who sent Him
- for judgment
- for people to have life and have it to the full
- as a light so that no-one who believed in Him should stay in darkness
- to give His life a ransom for many
- to set the captives free
- to confront not just confer

(Luke 12:51; John 6:5, 18:37; Matthew 5:17; Mark 1:38, 2:17; Luke 12:49; John 6:38, 9:39, 10:10, 12:46; Mark 10:45, 4:18).

Of course, you may think that these kinds of readings do not sound very 'Christmassy'. You are right. For starters, they are far too uncomfortable. There is not a single mention of straw and nothing here could be used as an advertising image for Baby Gap Christmas clothing. They elicit not 'ooh's' but 'ow's'. The fact of Christ's birth without the meaning is dumb. It is in the world's interest that we celebrate a dumb Christmas. However, for Christians, the four hundred years of prophetic silence prior to Christ's birth is not our heritage. Yet sadly, the dumbing-down has been successfully managed. The Christian message is re-baked with some self-help fattening ingredients, a lacing of self-affirming humanitarianism and sealed with some saccharine sentiment that has as much gospel power as damp smores.

As has been well discussed, originally the Christmas celebration was an attempt to provide a counter festival to the Roman one of the

Unconquerable Sun. So what began as a feast to Christianize a pagan festival has now gone full circle and become a festival that paganizes a Christian Feast. One can sympathize with the Puritans who felt that the only way to deal with the problem was either to drop out of the celebration or deny it altogether. Many would make a strong biblical case for those who abandon the materialistic mammon impulse and instead devote themselves and the money they would have spent, to mercy ministry among the poor. It is interesting that Paul, when writing to the Corinthians about their collections and offerings for distribution to the poor, sought to clinch the argument for the necessity of such ministry, by reminding them of a fundamental 'Christmas' point, or more correctly, of a non-negotiable understanding of the incarnation. They needed to follow the example of Jesus "who though He was rich, yet for your sakes became poor." Incarnational Christianity has a commitment to voluntary impoverishment on behalf of those who have been reduced to involuntary poverty. Of course, there are many who have abandoned the western seasonal modus operandi altogether and gone eastern, celebrating the Eastern Church's date for Christmas, namely Twelfth Night or Epiphany. This brings the focus back to the worship of the Magi and the manifestation of Jesus, not only first to His people the Jews, but also to the Gentiles as represented by the wise men.

Regardless of how we celebrate, let us at least celebrate. We could do no worse than celebrating both Christmas Day as well as Epiphany, and in doing so we will rejoice both in the fact that He came, and the reason why He came. The historical facts, earthed in the story of the birth narratives, and the theological reasons, grounded in the cross, resurrection, ascension and glorification of the son of Mary who always was the Son of God, when shaken and stirred, make a heady mix, that can only be expressed in an explosive doxology. The reverberating, pulsating praise takes its lyrics from the angelic choir that appeared to the shepherds: "Glory to God in the highest!" (Luke 2:14), and from the songs of the great multitude that gather around the throne in the Apocalypse: "Hallelujah! For the Lord God Almighty reigns! Let us rejoice and give Him glory!" (Revelation 19:6-7) And the tune? It is in the cadence of the music of "every tribe and language and people and nation" (Revelation 5:9).

Yes, from one perspective it might seem to some to be an irrational season, but from the viewpoint of the manger and the throne, it is the irrefutable season ... the irresistible season ... the irrepressible season ... precisely because it is the rational season.

The Synoptic and Apocalyptic Nativity

"... a virgin pledged to be married ..."
(Luke 1)

Shivering and shawled against the jet and jagged night
Woman on the cosmic catwalk, coutured by sun's light
Head-scarved in worn homespun, pinch-feet thonged in dank-dirt straw
Crowned with Virgo's constellation, spotlight moon her floor
Blank-gazed by dumb glazed and grazing parted hooves and cud
In her face gargoyled, gargantuan, dragon red as blood
Antiphons of seraphs, sages, shepherds – perfumed praise
Saw-toothed rage of serpent, Satan, pythoned paeans raise
Calloused, kindly hands soft-touch cheek-down so undefiled
Carnivored carnality waits to devour the child
Winged to safety by angelic pinioned, feathered grace
Snatched from claw and jaw of dragon to God's throne-thronged place
Tetrarch-terror abhors Ramah, aborts Rachel's birth
Monster-tail's Jurassic vengeance thrashes stars to earth
Out of Egypt came the Son, Beelzebub to bind
Out of heaven fell the reptile and his bestial kind
Glory be to God on high and on the earth be peace
Glory in God's heaven where our tears and curse will cease
My soul magnifies the Lord, I have not hoped in vain
Praise to Him who is and was, who has begun to reign!

"... a woman clothed with the sun ..."
(Revelation 12)
(1993)

134

Surprised by Joy

Regardless of all the threats, all the interruptions of normalcy, all the personal inadequacies of faith, all the impossibilities, all the sadness and badness, all the fear and failure, **JOY** just keeps bursting through the incarnation narrative, usually unprepared for, unexpected, and flashing like a diamond, like a sparkling shard of brilliant light. Have we not already noticed the threats that lurk in the narrative like landmines, discouraging the characters from trusting what is out there, and hindering their journey to where they should be going? It was a real battle. In wartime, the soldiers who are given the responsibility to both clear the landmines and repair the roads and bridges for a safe advance are called 'sappers'. Joy is God's sovereign sapper that not only clears the gloom and its causes, but also restores the hearts of the damaged and the broken. Suddenly, it breaks in, breaks out and breaks through.

Malcolm Muggeridge once testified, "I never knew what joy was until I gave up pursuing happiness." It is said that the word "happy" is derived from the word "happenstance" that describes whatever happens to be happening at that moment. So being happy is basically determined by a response to whatever is going on temporally and temporarily, which inevitably means it is likely to be transitory. Joy is of another order, for it is the affection of the eternal, not the ephemeral. We have already marked up all the threatening words in the narrative, so now, why not go through the text again and mark up every time that joy punches through the walls of despondency. (Why not put this book down and do that right now as a devotional exercise. You may even come back to this smiling!)

After centuries of national misery and after about 40 years of Zechariah's and Elizabeth's resigned sadness, the first thing Gabriel talks about is the "**joy** and delight" that their son is going to be to them and that "many will **rejoice** at his birth" (Luke 1:14). That came true as we read about the community's response to Elizabeth's delivery: "they shared her **joy**" (Luke 1:58). As soon as the pregnant Mary walked into the room of the pregnant Elizabeth, the unborn John somersaulted in the womb "for **joy**" (Luke 1:44). Already, joy was the instant and instinctual response to Jesus, always elicited when someone came into His gravitational field. Was that not what happened to the magi when the star stopped and they came to the house? "They were **overjoyed**" (Matthew 2:10). In the midst of all the threatening words that describe bad realities and daily bad news, the message from the angel of the Lord to the shepherds was direct: "I bring you good news of great **joy**" (Luke 2:10). The recovery is of joy, of the affections of an assured creature for the Creator, of lost sons and daughters for a found Father, of lost sheep for a Good Shepherd. Would Jesus not say later in His parable about the lost sheep, that when the shepherd finds it "he **joyfully** puts it on his shoulders" and is not the first thing that he says to his friends: "**Rejoice** with me" (Luke 15: 5-6)? What was the evidence of Mary's peace after being "troubled"? She tells us: "My spirit **rejoices** in God my Savior" (Luke 1:47).

Incontrovertibly, the Advent narrative reminds us that distress and suffering cannot disqualify us from experiencing the joy of the Lord. If our lives are governed only by how we respond to temporal circumstance, to how we are being treated, to what is being feared, to what is shaming us or disgracing us, to what is limiting or subverting us, then it will only be about a search for circumstantial happiness. But if our lives are governed by how we relate to who Jesus is, then as in the story, the bad news of circumstance has no power against the good news of great joy. Paul learned this: "In all our troubles, my **joy** knows no bounds" (2 Corinthians 7:4); "We **rejoice** in sufferings" (Rom. 5:3-5). James learned this: "Consider it pure **joy** when you face trials of many kinds" (James 1:2-3). Peter learned this: "**Rejoice** that you participate in the sufferings of Christ, so that you may be **overjoyed** when his glory is revealed" (1 Peter 4:13). So the suffering of circumstance actually invites us to be overjoyed at the prospect of God's work being perfected in us. The thermostat that determines the warmth of our affections is not the circumstances without, but the Christ within. It is the Emmanuel principle that if He is now with us, then we rejoice at His presence, and do not recoil at anything present that is inimical to our joy.

Meanwhile, this child was laying in a manger, seemingly oblivious to the real dangers around Him, dangers that were sufficient for the holy family to become refugees and flee to Egypt. Not only did the joy continue around Him, regardless, but also for the rest of His life, He continued in that joy. He would later teach His disciples exactly what His earthly parents and natal supporters had discovered: that opposing circumstance and enmity toward faith in Him could only draw one possible response from them: "**Rejoice** ... and leap for **joy**" (Luke 6:23). His life had been birthed in a time of grief but His arrival brought joy, so He could tell His disciples with authority that although there is real grief experienced amidst loss and persecution, it is never the final word: "your grief will turn to **joy**" (John 16:20). Is there any more luminous a moment in the gospels than when Jesus Himself is described as "full of **joy** through the Holy Spirit" (Luke 10:21)? Is it any surprise that the great joy of which the angelic host sang, would be what He longed for most for all who would receive that incarnational good news in the future? Is that not why He said He taught them, in order that their "**joy** may be complete" (John 15:11)? Was not His last recorded prayer for them "that they may have the full measure of my **joy** within them" (John 17:13)? And did He not go from that place of prayer to the cross, and despite the circumstantial suffering, was He not able to endure it and scorn its shame for "the **joy** that was set before Him" (Hebrews 12:2)? From the moment He rose again, joy was the affection of His community (Luke 24:41). After the Ascension, how extraordinary that the disciples returned to Jerusalem, not with tears, but "with great **joy**" (Luke 24:52). So it is no surprise that the consistent and continuing fruit of coming to Christ, as recorded in Acts, is "**joy** in the Holy Spirit" (13:52). The converted jailer represents all who have ever come to Jesus: he was "filled with **joy** because he had come to believe" (16:34).

The incarnation narratives are indeed an overture, tuning us for what is to come. Like all those in that story, we too choose, not just at Advent, but every day to "fix our eyes on Jesus" (Hebrews 12:2) and that is why, again like them, we can throw off every circumstantial thing that hinders and trips us, that burdens us, that smears and ensnares us, that disappoints and entangles us and interferes with our walk with Christ, especially our sin. Like Mary and Joseph, like Zechariah and Elizabeth, like the wise men and the shepherds, like Simeon and Anna, our eyes are not fixed on the jumble of personal perceptions and perspectives, or the jungle of inchoate anxieties and self-condemnations. Not only is our joy not diminished by all this distress, it is increased because more joy is obtained through triumphing over it.

The presentation of joy in the incarnation narratives is never just a private personal matter because when Gabriel tells Zechariah that he will experience joy, he adds, "many will rejoice." When Elizabeth's pregnant joy is known about, her neighbors "shared her joy." And that joy of hers, quickened by the joy of a visiting Mary, sets off joy in her unborn son. Mary's spirit that "rejoices" in God her Savior is not a solo performance, but is going to be expressed by all the generations who will be in the choir that call her blessed and share her joy. The "good news of great joy" that was announced to the shepherds was not for them alone in their splendid isolation but for "all the people". Because the joy was for everyone, they went and became the first evangelists of the New Testament, and "spread the word concerning what they had been told." If this joy had not been communal, had not been expressed, then Zechariah and Elizabeth would be closeted at home alone choosing baby clothes, the neighborhood would be going about their usual depressing and repetitive order of business, Mary would be a soloist whose song would be off the charts in a week, and the shepherds would still be telling depressing stories about their worst encounters with wolves. In the advent story, the spiritual joy of one is always the promotion of the joy of all.

May you experience the personal and communal joy of the Lord this Advent. I am not talking about a seasonal happiness that comes from socially explicable gatherings, whether family or church, but a fresh incarnational, transformational joy in your life and circumstances, the joy that is indeed unspeakable and full of glory. The theme of the poem that follows simply affirms what we have been talking about: that regardless of the litany of pain, joy has the final word. Indeed, joy to the world, the Savior's come!

Surprising Joy

"... living in darkness and the shadow of death ..."
(Luke 1:79)

Above the sunken hope the incense rose.
The silence of four hundred years screamed pain.
The worship could not hide the welts and woes
Of spirits crushed by godless Roman reign.
There was no reason for prayers to be bold,
This was no season for faith to be firm.
The expectation was just the same-old,
The future devoured by the canker worm.
But still the liturgy must be intoned,
Without a sense of being seen or heard.
Why would this priest believe God was enthroned?
There were no wonders and there was no Word.
　　"Your asking has been answered," spoke a voice.
　　*"He'll be a **joy** and many will **rejoice.**"*

Aaron's descendant, perfect pedigree,
In God's sight upright, keeping all the law,
Observing regulations blamelessly;
But if her heart was righteous, why so raw?
Because she had outpoured infertile tears,
Bearing her barrenness with public shame;
Because she was now well along in years,
And never would an infant get to name.
The brokenness of longing unfulfilled,

139

Stuart McAlpine

The loneliness of childless days and nights,
The sadness of a crib that was unfilled,
All sighed the loss of motherhood's delights.
　"Your wife, Elizabeth, will bear a boy."
　"The babe within my womb did leap for **joy**."

All was not calm, or gentle, mild and bright.
At first, there were no angels' songs to hark;
The peace was pricked with sharpened shards of fright.
Virginity seemed threatened in the dark.
And Bethlehem not quite so still did lie
As census-citizenry fought for beds;
And not so silent did the stars go by,
As visions tore the dreamless sleep to shreds.
Too young, too old, too sinful, just too bad;
The litany of threat, chillingly clear,
Too late, too shameful, too doubting, too sad;
Divorce, disgrace, disturbed, terrified, fear.
　"Be not afraid for I am God's envoy,
　I bring to you the good news of great **joy**."

My circumstances do disqualify
This one, in my mind, from your graciousness,
And convince and condemn me to deny
Deliverance from my unworthiness;
That I could be a player in your acts
Of incarnation, of your kingdom come.
I bow my knee and submit all the facts
Of my life to your generous wisdom.
And as at your Son's, my Christ's, promised birth
Let not my dire despair, or dull dismay

Obscure the revelation of His worth,
Obstruct the ending of my joy's delay.
"According to your Word will be my choice;
In Savior God my spirit will *rejoice!*"

"My spirit rejoices in God my Savior!"
(Luke 1:47)
(2015)

Christmas Contrariness

Christmas is a season of giddying disconnects, of serial contrariness. Has this happened again to you this year? You are in a public place, and Christmas music is being played in the background. Mariah Carey belts out "All I want for Christmas is you" and you have more than a sneaky suspicion that she is not talking about Jesus! But then she sings, "Joy to the World" and "Jesus is a wonderful child". I usually stand among other shoppers in disbelief that such truth had slipped through the cultural censor's net. But the fact is that we are bombarded with these seasonal disconnects:

- between the temporary public appearance of religious form and the reality of a rampant, private irreligion;
- between the virginity of the incarnation and the fornication of Christmas revelries and office parties;
- between heavenly choirs and drunken ones;
- between angels and elves;
- between holy-holy-holy and ho-ho-ho;
- between the supernaturalism of divine conception and the unbelieving naturalism of biological explanation;
- between the sanctity of a Savior's birth and the parental sentimentality of Santa's grotto;
- between the one who for our sakes became poor and the many who for their own sakes have determined to become rich;
- between the prophetic and the pragmatic;
- between the manger and the mall;
- between the single divine word made flesh and the volume of fleshly human verbiage;

- between the gift of salvation and our works of self-preservation;
- frankly a disconnect between heaven and earth.

When it comes to dissonances and disconnects, when it comes to contraries, the birth narratives are full of them. As in a good mystery, things are said that cannot be fully understood at the time; things happen that at first appear to be random. Until, that is, we watch the dots being sovereignly joined to flesh out an extraordinary visual of God, not just working among us, but also actually coming among us. We learn quickly in this story that God chooses and uses these characters regardless of how the contraries of their own lives ended up defining their view of themselves, and of reality: "I'm an old man ... I'm barren ... I'm a virgin ... I will divorce her." But when God shows up in their lives, how contrary is the revelation of an angel, the voice in the dream, the swelling belly, to what had been their previous experience. All of their negative, self-doubting, God-questioning self-designations are overcome by the inclusive grace of God that counts into His purposes those who had excluded themselves. As Zechariah puts it, they are overwhelmed by the tender mercies of God. He is still in the business of turning the graveyards of our dead expectations into the maternity wards of His purpose and will. He can take every initial response to His revelation (including our doubt, denial, disbelief, even dread) and impart the gift of faith.

Nothing looks good at first in this story; everything looks like one contrary mess, but as the text reminds us, it is not about our perceptions so much as it is about God's perspective. When He sees us as we really are, He sees nothing that is so contrary that it is beyond the power of His grace and love to integrate, to reconcile into His story. The fact is that Elizabeth needed more than a fertility clinic; Joseph needed more than a divorce attorney; and Mary needed more than a pregnancy test; and Zechariah needed more than a faith message to sort out their contraries. The shepherds needed more than an invitation from the mayor to get them into town, and the wise men needed more than Herod's help could give them. Thank goodness the opening volley from heaven in this story is the one we still need in the midst of all our contraries: 'Nothing is impossible with God!' The one who said, "I'm past it!" contrarily ended up saying "His name will be John!" The one who said "I'm out of here!" contrarily ended up saying "His name is Jesus!" The one who could have said, "The village will call me the local slut!" contrarily ended up saying, "All generations will call me blessed." God takes the contrariness out of the contrary, and He connects the disconnects. He makes of a piece what we saw as 'in pieces'. With amazement we watch God at work drawing people with no sense of worthiness or readiness into the center stage of His gorgeous will. God seems to delight in getting together with those who do not have it together. He seems to know how to reconcile what presents itself as irreconcilable.

Is there anything more contrary than light and darkness? But is that not what the prophet Isaiah turns on its head as he predicts the coming of Jesus: "The people walking in darkness have seen a great light; on those living in the land of the shadow of death, a light has dawned." What could have been more contrary to the inky blackness of sin, to the darkness of separation from God, to the national depression of 400 years, than the supernatural light display of "the glory of God in the highest" that broke through that incarnation-night. No one was singing, "Twinkle, twinkle little star." This was stupendously cosmic. And by the way, the baby grew to manhood and said amidst the darkness, "I am the light of the world." Is that not how John's gospel begins its announcement of Jesus' coming? Jesus is the true light that gives light to every person. Two chapters later, symbolically, Nicodemus comes to Jesus by night. Everyone knows John 3:16 but forgets what immediately follows: "Light has come into the world." And Jesus then tells us what this revelation of who He is and why He came, actually does: it reveals everything that is contrary – contrary to His will for us, to His creational design, to His loving intentions and longings towards us, to His future for us. "I have come into the world as a light so that no one who believes in Me should stay in darkness." None of us need live in the spiritual twilight zone, in a dawn that never breaks, in a spiritual dusk, in the shadow-lands. If you do feel like David the psalmist when he described himself as a cold and flameless candle, you can make his prayer your own: "You light my candle, my God. Turn my darkness into light" (18:28).

If Jesus' own explanation of why He came was to be the light in our darkness, then here is what we need to know more than anything else this Advent:

1. In our natural state, we are, to use Paul's words, "darkened in our understanding and separated from the life of God" (Ephesians 4:18). Darkness is our natural state no matter how we try to camouflage it with the illuminations of our own making.
2. Into this darkness came Jesus Christ, the light of the world, the revelation of the heart and character, the will and purpose of God for each one of us.
3. Each one of us, to experience the life God intended for us all along, must bring all of who we are, to all that Jesus is, and bring our darkness to His light, our sin to His forgiveness, our denial of responsibility for our sin to His acceptance to take responsibility for the atonement of that sin through His death on the cross (when incidentally, there was great darkness over the land).

According to Jesus, people can respond contrarily to the light in one of three ways:

- He says people shun it because their deeds are basically evil and they *"hate the light"* (John 3:20). This animosity is increasingly prevalent and calcifying in our culture and it is worse now than it was this time last year. Personal sin, the societal acceptance of what God has denied and condemned, is a far greater enemy of both the gospel and society than a political philosophy. Ideological Marxism is arguably a less virulent form of antichrist than the freewheeling, self-preferential, promiscuous paganism of that part of our society that hates the Christian gospel.
- He says that people *"fear the light"* (John 3:20) because it exposes who they really are under the covers. It is just too painful to have to come to terms with what goes on in the hidden basements of our souls.
- He says people just *"prefer darkness to light"* (John 3:19). They are pro-choice darkness. Eat, drink and be merry for tomorrow we die. Keeling over beats kneeling down. At least the Bible, and Jesus in particular, are utterly realistic. It declares that there is pleasure in sin, but it points out that the titillation of nerve ends and the

satisfaction of ego only lasts a short time. At the end of the day, we are going to have to deal with our contrariness.

And if these three responses of ours are not bad enough, the Bible teaches that the whole enterprise to stay in a world contrary to God's light, is funded and facilitated by a satanic personality: "the god of this world has blinded minds so they cannot see the light of the gospel of the glory of Christ who is the image of God" (2 Corinthians 4:4).

If Jesus were in our Advent services, what would He say in His homily in the candle-lit darkness? I think that He would repeat the three things that His light does when it comes to us this Christmas, just as it came that first Advent:

1. It **exposes** the darkness. Paul writes: "God will bring to light what is hidden in darkness and will expose the motives of our hearts" (1 Corinthians 4:5).
2. It **explains** the darkness. It reveals that my sin has separated me from relationship with God and kept me in the dark, ignorant of His life and light.
3. It **expels** the darkness, because wherever Christ's light shines, old darkness and bondages have to go (John 1:5). As John put it, the light shines in the darkness and the darkness cannot put it out, and has to pack up and move out.

One of the most common images in the New Testament for acknowledging the truth of why Jesus came, for acknowledging Jesus as our personal Lord and Savior, is the one that describes us as coming "out of darkness into His marvelous light" (1 Peter 2:9). To the Ephesians, Paul writes, "You were once darkness but now you are light in the Lord. Live as children of light and find out what pleases the Lord. Have nothing to do with the fruitless deeds of darkness" (Ephesians 5:8).

Isaiah spoke of those in darkness seeing a great light, and he was also the one who recognized that people would reject that light and try and light their own darkness. "Come on, baby, light my fire." Listen to his chilling words, that he actually puts in the mouth of the suffering servant, the Christ who is to come, who has come, whose coming we celebrate at Advent: "All you who light fires and provide yourselves with flaming torches, go, walk in the light of your own fires and of the torches you have set ablaze. This is what you shall receive … you shall lie down in torment" (Isaiah 50:11). O dear! Does anyone ever mention the word "torment" in their Christmas communication? Give us only jingling good cheer and warm us up for some optimistic thoughts for the New Year. Well, there is some good news. Isaiah contrasts two sources of light to deal with the darkness. What is the second one? "Let him who walks in the dark, who has no light, trust in the name of the Lord and rely on his God" (Isaiah 50:10).

Every Advent, contrariness is center stage again. Either we will accept, or re-affirm our acceptance of the light of God in Jesus Christ, or we will choose, contrarily, to deny that, or convince ourselves that we can enlighten ourselves or light our darkness with those self-lit, self-guided torches that take on so many forms: the light of our own intuition instead of the revelation of God's instructions; the light of our insights, imaginations, common sense, traditional or cultural values; the luminosity of our own accomplishments and achievements, our own smarts and self-worth, our own self-perceived sexual identities and successes; the sparks of our own ingenuity and experience; the fires of our own passions and wills. But in the end, if we fail to see the light that shone in the incarnation narrative and walk in it, we will at some point or other, be forced to lie down with the consequences of our own failed efforts at self-enlightenment. The choice is between a do-it-yourself approach to darkness, and a God-in-Jesus approach to light.

When we accept Jesus as God's gift of salvation an extraordinary thing happens. The light of the world turns round and says to us as He said to the disciples in His sermon on the mount, "You are the light of the world." God chooses to reveal who He is through us. We become luminaries as it were, which is why Paul told the Philippians that in a dark generation they were called to "shine like stars" as they offered others the word of life. So at Advent time, it is not just about "the stars in the bright sky." Advent is about us determining again to be like Jesus, who John simply described as a witness to the light. This alone make sense of all the contrariness, because in His light we see light. When it comes to contrariness and Christmas, the words of Phillip Brooks in the carol 'O little town of Bethlehem' have it about right:

> Yet in thy **dark streets shineth**
> The Everlasting **Light**;
> The **hopes** and **fears** of all the years
> Are met in Thee tonight.

Mary, Mary, Quite Contrary

"Mary was greatly troubled."
(Luke 1:29)

First one thing now another, it feels like touch and go,
It's a sure thing, or is it; it's yes and then it's no.
It's rightly then it's wrongly; it's black and then it's white.
The pendulum keeps swinging, it's darkness then it's light.
It's hemming and it's hawing, it's sharp or is it flat?
It can be all or nothing; it's neither this nor that.
It's all sixes and sevens, it's running hot and cold;
It's way more closed than open, were the truth to be told.
It's perfect then it's past it, it's off but should be on;
It's certain then it's curtains, it's true then it's a con.
Between a rock and hard place, here one day gone the next;
Euphoric with the blessing, then feeling it's been hexed.
It's swimmingly ecstatic, then drowning in the tide;
This morning, seeds were growing, this evening they had died.
What's possible went AWOL, sad mumble doused glad shout;
What's personal went viral; it's neither in nor out.
I thought that it was worth it, or was it just a waste;
It's fork-tongued, double-minded, no wonder it's two-faced.
I used to peal with laughter, and now the joke's on me;
My hope in terra firma has just gone out to sea.
Transparency was valued, but now it's clear as mud.
Once covenant meant something - now can't trust my own blood.
It's promised then it's broken, it's neither up nor down,
What's silent was once spoken, the rags were once a gown.

149

Are those cheeks creased with laughter, or wrinkled with despair?
If justice rolled like rivers, why is life so unfair?
This face pressed on the hard floor, was headfirst in the clouds;
One minute I was bridal, the next I'm choosing shrouds.
Today's joy will be grief soon, disguised by a brave face;
What was known as amazing, is now amusing grace.
Reality's appearance now keeps the facts unseen;
And between you and me, dear, all's betwixt and between.

(Mary, Mary, quite contrary, how does the story go?)

Four centuries of silence, a lung-loud heavenly host;
The lost and last and little, now used by God the most.
The demons racked the country, but angels packed the skies.
Magnificat asserted the truth in face of lies.
The humble were exalted, the proud were brought to ground;
The outcast was invited, the lost were now the found.
The rich go away empty, the hungry eat their feast,
Athens and Rome are by-passed, Ephrathah was the least.
The barren is now pregnant, the virgin is with child,
The arrogance of empire, displaced by meek and mild.
For disgrace there was favor, and faith overcame fears;
The one who asked was answered, the blind became the seers.
Those up the creek went mainstream, the terrified found calm.
Woes were replaced by worship, the song-less found their psalm.
A womb was Spirit-seeded, a spirit pierced by sword;
The empty cribs of Ramah, the mangered babe adored.
The Magi searched to worship, while Herod sought to kill,
The days were rowdy-riddled, that night was quite stone-still.
While some were warned by visions, others were wooed by star.
Those who were near knew nothing, the wise came from afar.
Though poverty was pounding, those precious gifts did sign,
That priceless was the treasure that now was yours and mine.
The land in death's dark shadow, received the rising sun,
The prophecies once pending, were now fulfilled deeds done.
The longing and the weeping, heard good news of great joy;

The jaws of Satan's kingdom, smashed by a toothless boy.
Could it be that our ledgers of worldly solvency,
Are really just recording spiritual bankruptcy?
Could it be that regardless of how sin's debit looks,
That this child would be able to reconcile the books?
Indeed it is contrary, the story of this child.
Could it be our contraries in Him are reconciled?

(Mary, Mary, quite contrary, how did the story go?)

"My soul glorifies the Lord!"
(Luke 1:46)
(2016)

His Birth, My Death

Christ's birth and my death? What has morbidity to do with seasonal merriment? What on earth has this got to do with Christmas? In a word, everything. It is hardly the most popular subject for an Advent meditation but many people cannot bear too much reality on such occasions it seems. A few years ago I was teaching an expositional series on First Thessalonians and it overlapped into Advent. I realized that there was no need to take a break in favor of a more custom-made Advent series. Why? Paul was addressing the status and future of those who had "fallen asleep" and he was not referring to those who, like Eutychus, had dropped off during one of his long messages, following a strenuous time of worship. So how does this qualify as a Christmas theme? What possible relationship is there between a manger and a coffin? Why would cemeteries ever be mentioned at Christmas?

Writing to the Corinthians, Paul put it this way: "Since death came through a man, the resurrection of the dead comes also through a man. For as in Adam all die, so in Christ, all will be made alive" (1 Corinthians 15:21-22). Paul is explaining why those who have "fallen asleep" are not lost. He stresses the humanity of Christ in his answer. For Jesus to pioneer our salvation He had to become as we were; He had to be born. He came as the last Adam. Sin came through one man, and death through sin and consequently death came to all people (Romans 5:12). But as the last Adam, the one man Jesus became the progenitor of a new humanity, and this was sealed by His resurrection. Whatever He achieved became available and achievable for everyone who would be reconciled to Him, or to put it in seasonal terms, receive the most incredible gift imaginable. Jesus used the language of gift giving during His ministry. He presented

Himself as "living water" to the Samaritan woman as "the gift of God" (John 4:10).

When we say at Christmas that Jesus is the "indescribable gift" (2 Corinthians 9:15), that is true, but the gift that Paul is talking about is not just Jesus in His baby clothes. The gift can only be fully unwrapped and understood when Jesus does some unwrapping of His own and steps out of His grave-clothes, alive and well. The gift He gives, that He was born to give, was salvation. Was that not what the angel told Joseph? "He will save His people from their sins" (Matthew 1:21). Paul describes this gift as "the gift that came by grace" and "the gift of righteousness" (Romans 5: 15, 17); as "the gift of eternal life" (Romans 6:23); as "the gift of God", salvation "by grace … through faith" (Ephesians 2:8).

Paul calls Jesus the first-fruits of those who have been raised from the dead. The first-fruits was that initial offering of the harvest that served notice that there was lots more to come. In the same way, the first fruit of the resurrection of Jesus from the dead is the proof that our resurrection is settled if we are reconciled to Him. There is a harvest of resurrections to follow His. In Adam we were born once. In Christ we were born again. In Adam, we had natural descent and we will all die. In Christ, we have supernatural descent and all who are born again will be made alive.

So why is this at all important at Advent? What do answers about the future hope of dead people have to do with a celebration of the incarnation? This is why it is so precious and meaningful to participate in Christmas Communion. The remembrance of Christ's death is not incompatible with the remembrance of Christ's birth. It is not enough to talk about an occupied manger that states the fact that He came. Of course, we must do that, and we boldly declare that Christ came in the flesh. However, we must also talk about an unoccupied tomb that states the meaning of it all. His birth delivery is unto our deliverance from the power of sin and death, so that having been born once and begun immediately to die, we may be born again so that we may live with Him forever. Are you still feeling morbid? Is this not pure joy? Happy Christmas indeed!

What follows is a poem that I wrote to express this truth. It will not strike you at first as very 'adventy', but I hope that by the time you get to the end of it you will realize that it is as seasonal as Paul's teaching on bereavement. It might also help you to know that I wrote this poem in the advent season of a year in which I had been seriously ill with a life-threatening affliction, and I had reason to consider my mortality as a descendant of Adam, and therefore my immortality as a descendant of Jesus Christ. May you know the unwrapped risen Christ this Advent!

Transposition by Transfusion

"For as in Adam all die ..."

I lay dark-hospiced in my coffined cot,
My morphined soul oblivious to all.
The needled veins of feeling long since dry,
Infected by self-aided will.
Terminal.
Imminent death.
You sent me no condolences,
No hallmarked greetings for trite miracles;
No inter-floral sentiments
To fragrance decomposing hope,
And wish me unwell to my eye-shut wake.

Instead, you lay light-strobed in stabled crib,
Divinity unobvious to all.
The jugular of deity flowed full,
Untainted and infection-free.
Eternal.
Immaculate birth.
That by your blood my life could be transfused,
And in an instant be transformed
From grave-bands to your swaddling cloth,
To be newborn again, wide-eyed awake.

I bid you therefore cease your last-breath sighs,
And give voice to a newborn baby's cries.
He is the second Adam from on high,
And all who have His blood will never die!

"... so in Christ shall all be made alive."
(1 Corinthians 15:22)
(1999)

The Advent of Asking

There is a lot of asking that goes on in the birth narratives. The text is about two main things:

- *what God asks of those in the story:* "You are to give him the name John ... You will be with child ... Take Mary home as your wife because what is conceived in her is from the Holy Spirit ... Take the child and his mother and escape into Egypt ... A sword will pierce your own soul ..."
- *what people in the story ask of God:* "The assembled worshippers were praying outside ... your prayers have been heard ... Simeon ... was waiting for the consolation of Israel ... Anna ... worshiped night and day, fasting and praying ..."

But just to complicate things a little, you cannot read this narrative without realizing that there are two other possible categories:

- *what these people get that they did not ask for:* "Mary ... You will be with child ... Joseph ... She will give birth to a son ..." Was this an answer to prayer for either of them? "Dear God, please may I conceive before I get married!"
- *what they then ask about what they get:* "How can I be sure of this?" "How will this be?"

The fact is that if our spiritual blessings were premised only on our asking of God, some of us would not be very blessed at all. The grace of God, precisely because it is not about our merits, seems to give and give and give again, sustaining and providing, blessing and protecting, providing and supporting so far beyond the projection of our asking, and absolutely beyond our deserving. This is first a story about what God asks of people: of a young Mary, an unknown Joseph, a rustic Zechariah, and a disappointed Elizabeth. Faith was asked of the wise men, trust was asked of the shepherds. Patience was asked of Simeon and Anna. We should be undone and humbled by the asking of God of us, by the divine invitation that would come to us and ask us, unfitted as we are like the players in this story, to participate in His plans, to be partners in His ventures, to be co-workers in his mission.

This particular Advent, despite the myriad of things we may be well-versed in asking, and maybe really need to ask for, would it perhaps be good for us to ask God what He would ask of us? Maybe we just need to stop and look and listen to what He is asking. The chances are that some of what He is asking is way beyond our comfort level, way beyond our faith level, way beyond our ability or gifting level. So much the better! What He asks of us is His loving way to invite us into a fresh relationship of dependency, co-operation and intimacy with Him, where our first response to His asking is to ask Him a question, simply because we have so little to bring to the project. God loves these conversations with us. We always think that our prayers, by virtue of their asking for something, initiate the conversation. Not so. Our asking is not only at His invitation; it is a response to an initiative He has already made, which is why our asking is really an answering to God, to what He has already said. It would be wonderful to be the kind of humble and trustworthy people like Mary and Joseph, who would be those that God could ask things of; that like them, despite our limitations, we would be totally accessible to God, totally available. O to be thus favored!

But this is a story in which God is indeed asked for things. It begins: "Your prayers have been answered" (Luke 1:13). What had they asked for? As we have already discussed, the two prayers that are possibly referred to here were both going to be answered in the same divine plan: a Messiah for Israel and a baby for Elizabeth. There is plenty of other asking that goes on: Simeon and Anna, persevering, faithful and actually totally expectant, never succumbing to bitterness as the years rolled by, never allowing the lack of an answer and therefore the necessity of continued asking, to stop them fulfilling what God had given them to do and made them to be. Despite the realities of aging, their asking seemed to engender more faith and fervor. There is something in the perseverance of the asking that is in itself purifying and empowering, even in the face of possible discouragement. Maybe I could put it this way. Asking that is wearying and discouraging, is only strengthened and emboldened through continued asking.

Then there were those things that they got that they did not ask for. How many times have you said to God, "I didn't ask for this!" But the fact is you have got it. For every bad thing there are scores of good things that we equally did not ask for specifically but which yet litter the circumstances of our lives on a daily basis. Most of God's grace toward us is unasked for. Believe me, Mary's pregnancy was a very bad thing for Joseph who did not yet understand what God would work and purpose through it, anymore than you and I know what God intends to do through our inconvenient and downright subversive circumstances. Yet consider all the grace and favor toward Mary that she never asked for.

It is important to acknowledge this lest we think that we only receive because we ask. God wants us to ask, invites us to ask, but His giving to us is not controlled by that. The fact is that because God loves us, He gives and gives and gives again, unstintingly, and like a good parent, even when we are like undeserving and brattish children. Have you noticed that if you love someone, then you just love him or her to ask things of you as a way to show your love to them? I might add that there is almost humor in those occasions when we ask for something and eventually get it and find that we are experiencing more challenges in being answered than we were unanswered. Think of Rebekah who prayed for a child for twenty years and when she eventually was answered found she had twins that were wrestling in her womb. Pre-natally, it was not a comfortable answer to prayer, and it got worse post-natally as the answers that were Esau and Jacob presented challenges to faith and family.

Finally, the last possible category I mentioned had to do with the asking of God that we end up doing about what we do get that we did not ask for, whether good or bad. Have you ever asked, Why me? What have I done to deserve this? What does this mean? Where is God? Or have you ever had an encounter with God that has so refreshed and cleansed you, so encouraged and equipped you that you end up asking questions that want to know if it is too good to be true or to be believed? Or will it last? Have you ever been given a provision or promise or prophecy out of left

Stuart McAlpine

field and asked about your worthiness, or asked about when it will happen, or if it is possible? Is it reliable? Can it be trusted? In your own way, you have been where Mary and Joseph found themselves. You have been where Zechariah's faith ran out of road and the doubt came flooding in, and with it unbelief. God does not quench our asking. We should be amazed at His forbearance and patience with us as we doubt, and we pout and demand and impugn Him. But we need to be sensitive to the fact that not all our questions of Him are appropriate. There is a world of difference between Zechariah's "How can?" and Mary's "How will?"

What you must learn from this story is that there are many ways that our expectation gets beaten down, and consequently, our asking is reduced to formulaic, faithless, liturgical prayers like the one Zechariah was praying for Israel; or our asking is discouraged by the way we inventory the prevailing conditions of our circumstances – the hindrances and obstacles of our versions of being old and barren, or young and a virgin. Of course these conditions can persuade us to stop asking altogether because we have now learned to suppress expectation and accommodate resignation and rationalize loss and lack. Maybe we have raised another line of inquiry. Are we always as prepared for the answers to our asking as we pretend to be, or think we are? What cannot be denied is that the birth of Jesus recovers asking, after a time when there appeared to be no answers. It is interesting to note that right before His death, in His very last communication with His disciples in the Upper Room, He tells them again and again, to continue to ask in His Name. Jesus came to secure our asking of the Father, and He now ever lives to make intercession for us. What an Advent blessing that turned out to be.

160

Finding Father

"The God and Father of our Lord Jesus Christ ..."
(Romans 15:6)

FOR GOD the childless night was timeless long.
His pierced heart wept for offspring who **SO LOVED**
Themselves, and did not think **THE WORLD** of Him.
So could it be **THAT HE** would turn His back
On prodigals who **GAVE** such father-wounds?
How would **HIS** pained yet passioned patience bear
But **ONE** more spurned, ignored, rejected day?
Would unrequited **AND** paternal need
ONLY be satisfied should He adopt
A **SON** or daughter from another seed?
Where is **THAT** orphanage that could supply
Such Abba love? **WHOEVER,** once disowned,
Once branded illegitimate, **BELIEVES**
IN hope of being chosen, born again?
Should we not privy-pity **HIM** or her,
And brand "abandoned" those who **WILL NOT** be
(**PERISH** the thought) ever in family,
BUT live as slave and illegitimate,
Resigned till death to **HAVE** no filial joy;
Unfathered, for an **EVERLASTING** age
And unclaimed in their death as in their **LIFE**?

*"How great is the love the Father has lavished on
us, that we should be called children of God!"*
(1John 3:1)
(2011)

Going Home

We have come to the end of the overture. That word in English, remember, comes from the French 'ouverture', which means 'opening'. So we are now at the closing of the opening. But the opening to what, or more precisely, for whom? The overture comes at the beginning of the main work, the main piece of music, but the many elements that it contains are foreshadowing what is to come. So it is time to put this book down (thank you for getting this far!) and to pick up the New Testament that reveals what follows. If you have read this book at Advent season, then you are set up for the New Year to wander firmly into the glories of the rest of the Gospels and Epistles, all the way to the firework extravaganza at the very end, the book of Revelation. As you journey, you will come across so many of the 'overture' truths that we have already encountered in the incarnation narratives.

So what is "going home" all about? Listen to the text: "When his time of service was completed, he *returned home* … Mary stayed with Elizabeth for three months and then *returned home* … the shepherds *returned* … Joseph took Mary *home* … When Joseph and Mary had done everything required by the Law of the Lord, they *returned* to Galilee to their own town of Nazareth … they *returned* to their country by another route." That covers the wise men, Joseph, Mary and Jesus, the shepherds, and Zechariah. We know that Elizabeth was at home, and we assume that Anna just stayed in the Temple as she had done all those years, no doubt continuing to pray for the redemption of Israel.

There have been a lot of extraordinary miracles in this story: personal, national, global, and cosmic. One of the most precious of miracles is the way that these players in God's great drama, after all the trouble and turbulence, the confusions and fears, the shocks and shakes, are able to go home. They had all heard a lot and seen a lot, but the miracle is that they were all able to go home and work it out and work it in to their daily lives. After reading this overture, why not do the same. There have been lots of challenges, lots of applications, lots of questions, lots of responses, and lots of possibilities. Take everything to heart, but as Joseph counseled us, let us take it home, where we can let it all be to us according to God's Word that we have shared together. We need to work it out at home, in the interior rooms of our lives. As someone once said, "If it does not work at home, do not export it." We want to be able to witness to what God has done for us with integrity and authority.

There is one character in the story that was not mentioned above as returning home. However, I think he went home for sure. After he had played his role for God in this story, God just took him home to Himself, to his eternal home. Simeon asked God to do exactly that, did he not? I have not done a meditation on Simeon because I have saved it for the final poem. His last prayer is the last word of this overture, looking forward to the Advent that is to come. The advent story is both overture and adventure. Thank you for joining me. To borrow Simeon's words, may the Lord now dismiss all of us from this time together with each other in the story … in peace. Listen to Simeon as he prays for the last time … and goes home.

Simeon's Last Prayer

"He was waiting for the consolation of Israel."
(Luke 2:25)

How dear to me, my Lord, have been these temple courts,
Where like an aging virgin I ached pregnant thoughts;
Soft-wept for consolation by cold, wailing walls,
And mouthed mute hope in stone-deaf slabbed and silent halls.
Here corn-stalk arms were sunward stretched in harvest prayers,
And dammed up visions cataracted in blind stares.
In this your house I shuffled with flat-footed pace,
To plead for heaven's high-arched fleet and fluid grace.
My furrowed brow by bladed longing was deep-ploughed,
And plumb-lined plans and sky-rise dreams were spine-bent bowed.
Here wrinkled righteousness, and brittle-boned belief,
Age-spotted purity, have sought promised relief.
For was it not within this cloistered cell, your breath
Whispered that I would be made well before my death?

How dear to me, my Lord, have been my childless tears,
Yet sorrow was receding with advancing years,
Until that ebb-tide day when grief was spent at last,
And purchased for my soul the feast to end my fast.
Your Spirit, like a midwife calling closest kin,
Led me to the Father's house, bid me enter in.
I held your darling seed, then as grandfathers do,
Rejoiced as if he were my one and only too.
Of course, my Lord, I did not want to let him go.

Could I live on, perchance, to watch my Savior grow?
Ah me! Mumbling desire and fumbling need forgive!
You kept your word. I saw my Christ. You let me live.
Now I have seen your Son in this most holy place,
Dismiss your servant, Lord, to see His Father's face.

*"Now dismiss your servant in peace. For my eyes
have seen your salvation."*
(Luke 2:29-30)
(1994)

About the Author

The Apostle John inspired Stuart's desire to be both pastor and poet. A graduate of Cambridge University in English Literature and Theology, Stuart taught Literature before being called into pastoral ministry. He planted Christ Our Shepherd Church in Washington DC in 1987, where he continues to serve. Together with his wife Celia, he serves as the International Director of ASK Network (www.asknetwork.net), an international prayer movement, and also as a Senior Teaching Fellow at the C.S.Lewis Institute (www.cslewisinstitute.org). This book expresses his passions for the incarnation narrative, biblical meditation and poetry, expressed over thirty years of pastoral teaching on the birth narratives of Jesus. With creativity and imagination, Stuart has transmuted his annual Advent meditations into poems that illuminate the incarnation from fresh perspectives and invite us to relate in new ways to the Nativity story at the Christmas season.